A Friendly Community

A History of Middleport, New York

Anna B. Wallace

Images have been provided by a number of sources. Each image is identified by its source, indicated below:

Bonnie Witt
Buffalo newspaper (unidentified), circa 1910
Family of Tom Sheldon
Harold Mufford
HTH - Hartland Town Historian
Joe Ognibene and Tri-Town Ambulance
Lockport Union Sun and Journal
Mary B. Davenport
Medina Journal Register
Mrs. Grace Darroch
MVH- Middleport Village Historian
Patt Fagan
RHCL - Royalton-Hartland Community Library
RTH - Royalton Town Historian
Ruth Wallace Dorr
Sanford & Company 1878 Illustrated History of Niagara
    County
William Holahan Collection

The image on the cover is a painting by Myrtle Wilmot titled "Middleport on the Erie Canal, Batavia Preserving Company."

Image selection and placement by Christa Lutz.

Book design by Mike Miller, pubyourbook@gmail.com.

ISBN-13: 978-1523994557
ISBN-10: 152399455X

Table of Contents

Foreword

When I was appointed Village Historian in 1980, a friend said that she hoped that I would get around to writing a history - and I finally have gotten to it! As I started with an "empty box," I knew that it would take some time before I learned that much, although I had always been interested in local history. And I still don't know "everything."

I am indebted to Bill Holahan for his generous help when I had a question that I needed help with. He had been a "local historian" for many years, but when Middleport had to have a duly appointed historian, he was an elected trustee, and couldn't fill both posts. We had often "kibitzed" about old Middleport, and he presented my name for consideration. Also, then Town of Royalton Historian Donald Jerge was very helpful, and gave me copies of large quantities of Middleport-related material.

I have tried to be as accurate as possible with my information, and have purposely not used all of the dates that I have! Any omissions are not intentional, and I know that everything has not been covered, but what I record depends on the material that is available. I have gleaned information from many old newspapers and material that people have been kind enough to give to the office; even after all this time, there are many old papers at the library that I have not been able to read. This will at least cover most of the high spots of our prior years. But it is easier to find old material than the relatively current.

Many thanks to my husband for his patience with the continual state of chaos on my work table as I pored over papers and books. But it has been a volunteer labor of love!!

Anna Brewer Wallace

A Tribute to Anna Wallace

I had the pleasure of knowing and working with Anna Wallace, our (retired) Village of Middleport Historian for more than three decades until 2010. During my ten-year tenure as Mayor I could always depend on Anna's meticulous reports that were submitted annually to the Village and looked forward to reading our "history" as it unfolded year after year. Anna's congenial nature and conscientious work ethics made her an excellent choice for the position of Village Historian and she enthusiastically accepted my request to keep her position each year as part of the Village's re-organization process. For this, I was eternally grateful!

On a personal level, Anna and I share a birth date, November 23, and had many heartfelt conversations about our "date" when the church we both attended, Middleport United Methodist, held the annual Birthday Potluck celebration where we sat with those born in the same month. Those conversations proved that we had a lot of things in common … both married to businessmen, lived in Middleport our entire adult lives, members of the same church and we both shared an appreciation for history. Knowing of her love of Middleport and wanting to keep its history alive, I commend Anna for authoring this book and working with our current Village Historian, Christa Lutz, to get it published.

Thank you Anna for helping to keep Middleport's history alive and well.

Julie Maedl - Retired Mayor of Middleport

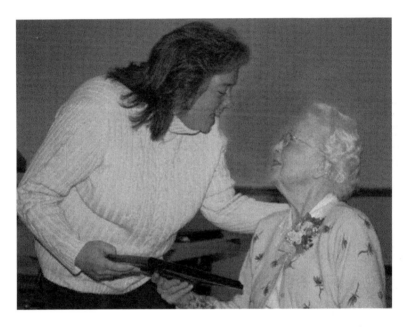

Mrs. Anna Wallace receiving a special proclamation from Jennifer Bieber, then deputy supervisor for the Town of Royalton, at her retirement.
(Image from RTH)

About The Cover

The cover of this book is a painting by Myrtle Wilmot, showing the Erie Canal looking towards the east with the Batavia Preserving Company on the north bank of the canal, the lift bridge and a rear view of the village buildings along Main Street.

Myrtle with her father, Elgie

Myrtle Lewis Wilmot was the daughter of Middleport resident and inventor Elgie J. Lewis and his wife, May Bathrick Lewis. Born in 1888, she attended Middleport High School, where she graduated in 1904, and then she went on to study music at the Julliard School of Music in New York City. She and her husband, Arthur M. Wilmot, lived most of their married life here on Terry Street and were active members of the Universalist Church and many other civic organizations.

In a newspaper article from 1972, Mrs. Wilmot was quoted that she took up painting when a local art class needed new members. She had never had any formal training but often admired scenes, thinking they might make a good picture. She would spend the next twenty years of her life painting scenes mostly of local interest.

Today many of her works can be found in the collection of the Royalton Hartland Community Library and the Village Hall in Middleport. Mrs. Wilmot lived until 1974 and after the passing of Mr. Wilmot in 1975, the major portion of their estate was left in trust to numerous educational, religious, health and civic organizations.

Early Settlers

When the settlers from the East came to their new homes, they most often came with a cow tied to the rear of their ox-drawn covered wagon, and just as often carried a crate of chickens. Thus milk, butter and eggs were available most of the year.

The pioneers who came to this area in 1806 settled on Route 31, east of Griswold Street. The community was called "Windsor," no doubt as they came from the Green Mountain County of Windsor, Vermont, as many of the settlers in this area did. The first settler of record is James Lyman who located in the area of Griswold Street and Telegraph Road. The property was later purchased by the Bennington family, who owned it for many years.

James Lyman was elected Supervisor of the (then) Town of Hartland in 1812 to replace E. Waldo who had died, and was re-elected again in 1816. When he offered land for sale in 1822, it was listed as being located "on the main road from Ellicott's Mills, through Slayton Settlement, and in the vicinity of Windsor."

James and Eunice Lyman were accompanied by James Williams, a blacksmith, who married their daughter Sally, and they became parents of a well-known local family. They are all buried in the old "Green Burying Ground," now Mountain Ridge Cemetery, on the Royalton

Center Road. Gravestones indicate that James Williams' parents, Ira and wife, came from Hartland, Windsor County, Vermont, to settle in Royalton in 1817.

Asher Freeman cabin, located on the northwest corner of Freeman and Mountain Roads.
(Image from RTH)

Our next settler of record is Asher Freeman who purchased 500 acres from the Holland Land Company in 1811, located a mile south of Middleport, "south of Lyman's and west of Babcock's," coming in from the south "by the marked black walnut trees." He came back to make his home here in 1815. He was one of three assessors elected at the first town meeting held in the Town of Royalton when the town was formed in 1817. Freeman was justice of the peace, and served three terms as Supervisor.

He was a frugal man, and by successive purchases eventually owned 1000 acres of land. He married in Washington County and had five sons; after he was widowed, he married again and had three sons and three daughters. He died at the age of 79.

William Ewing settled southwest of Middleport in 1814, selling to Joseph Odell, and then relocated a half-mile south of Middleport on the southeast corner of Main Street and Route 31. The original Ewing home had fallen on disrepair and was demolished in 1988. Prior to the birth of their daughter at Freeman's Corners in 1816, William Taylor purchased 400 acres of land from the Holland Land Company, coming here from New Jersey.

In 1815 Joseph Odell purchased 225 acres from the Holland Land Company, and owned a saw mill on the Mountain Road. Chauncey McKie settled on Griswold Street just north of the Lewiston Road, and Eliphalet Edmunds and John Griswold lived nearby. John and his family were buried in the old Ketchum Cemetery on Griswold Street.

Within ten years of the settling at Windsor, quite a trade center had grown at the four-corners, a local gathering place for the residents. Over the years this area was called by many different names: Pucker, Peeneyville, Tea Pot Hollow; and Barlow's Corners, Taylor's Corners, Ewing's Corners, Tucker's Corners, and Freeman's Corners for the people who lived there.

In 1816 Benjamin Barlow kept a tavern, the following year a distillery and an ashery, and was extensively engaged in the manufacture of potash. Advertising as a Farmers Store, he kept a "small assortment of domestic and English dry goods and groceries," and "will receive most kinds of produce and ashes in payment." He would also "exchange good whiskey for grain delivered" to his distillery. An agent for the Lockport Observatory, payment for the newspaper subscriptions could be made in wheat, corn or oats. The first member of the Assembly from Niagara County under the Constitution of 1821 was Benjamin Barlow, Jr., in 1823.

Asa Scott carried on a blacksmithing business at Barlow's Corners. Practically every household had at least one horse, so blacksmiths were necessary, not only for shoeing horses, but for making nails and other hardware, and for fixing machinery. The blacksmith was the forerunner of the present-day service station operator.

The earliest resident physician in this area was Dr. Benjamin H. Packard, locating southwest of Middleport, now the area of Manor Lane, in 1817. He was one of three Commissioners of the Common Schools elected at the first meeting in the Town of Royalton in 1818, and was one of three from the Town appointed in 1824 to "raise funds for the suffering Greeks." He came here from Royalton, Vermont, and stayed for about ten years before moving on to Ann Arbor, MI. Continuing his interest in education in 1835, he and two Methodist minister friends became founders of Albion College at Albion, MI. Today, Albion

College is a Methodist related liberal arts co-ed college with an enrollment of about 1900 students.

In a newspaper article about the Firemen's Ball, "the first ball ever held in this place or vicinity was in 1819 at Pucker's Corners now Freeman's and Ewing's Corners, when they had to go up to the second story on a ladder to get to the ballroom, the house standing on the northeast corner." This would be the location of 101 S. Main Street.

After the location of the canal had been decided, businesses began to spring up to be near "where the action would be."

Around 1820 Levi Cole opened a hotel in a little log house that was the beginning of Middleport village, the southeast corner of Main and State Streets. Later he changed locations and built a frame house on the opposite corner.

We have a copy of an invitation to the "Independence Ball, in commemoration of the Friend of Washington, our Nation's Guest, Lafayette!!" on July 5th, 1825, "at L. Cole's Assembly-Room in the Village of Middleport, at 10-clock P.M." This was before the canal was officially opened.

Front and back of the invitation for the Independence Ball in honor of Lafayette, a friend of George Washington during the Revolution. (Image from MVH)

The first homicide at Middleport was committed by Levi Cole, while the canal was being built. A party of workmen were in his tavern one evening becoming somewhat noisy from the too free use of firewater and indulging in language not generally used by sober men. Mrs. Cole was insulted. The ensuing melee carried out into the street, and as he was being pursued, Cole picked up a club and killed the man pursuing him, and seriously injured another. He was finally sent to State Prison for a short time for the deed.

In 1820 or 1821, Smith & Calkins did a large blacksmithing business at Middleport.

James Northam was the first merchant, starting business in 1822 where Main Street crosses the canal. At the time the canal had not been built, but the trees along the route had been cut and the brush piled for burning.

The Mather brothers erected a tannery here in 1824. That year Morning Sun Lodge #377, F&AM, was chartered with 11 Masons from the Middleport area. Benjamin Packard was charter Master; Elijah Mather, Jr., Warden; and Levi Cole was a charter member. The lodge relinquished its charter during the anti-Masonic years.

97 Main Street, the home built by William Taylor of dolomite limestone in 1825.
(Image from RTH)

William Taylor, who owned all the land in southeast Middleport east of Main Street and south of the canal, owned the second house north of the corner, at 97 S. Main Street. The Greek Revival style home was built in three different periods, 1825-1830, and is constructed of dolomite limestone from the cellar excavation and from Jeddo Creek next door. The cellar floor is of natural rock.

The tall white house on the southwest corner of Main Street and Route 31 is the former F. B. Freeman home, and in the late 1940s was the "Tree Lawn Tower" dining room. The large white house on the northwest corner, recently "The Shops at Teapot Hollow" is the former Philip Freeman home, reported to have been a station on the Underground Railroad. Linus Freeman built the brick house on State Street that is Bates, Wallace & Heath Funeral Home, Inc. All these Freemans were grandsons of early settler Asher Freeman. There are still descendants living in the area.

RES. OF F. B. FREEMAN. TOWN OF ROYALTON, NIAGARA CO., N. Y.

The F.B.Freeman home, drawn by an anonymous artist for a book on the early history of Niagara County. The house is still standing on the southwest corner of Main St. and Route 31.
(Image from the Sanford & Company 1878 Illustrated History of Niagara County)

The Phillip Freeman home on the northwest side of Main and Route 31, reportedly a stop on the Underground Railroad. As "Country House Furniture," it was a popular destination for couples looking to furnish their home. (Image from Bonnie Witt)

Arunah Bennett owned the land on the west side of Main Street, south of the canal; Gad Mather, the east side of Vernon Street, north of the canal; and F.B. Lane, the west side of Vernon Street, north of the canal.

Previously an unbroken wilderness area, the coming of the Erie Canal brought the business from Barlow's Corners to what is now "downtown" Middleport. The village received its name because of its location, midway between Lockport and Freeport, now Albion, the "middle" port in this section.

Clinton's Ditch or The Erie Canal

It has been said that more has been written about the Erie Canal than any other one topic in New York State except for Niagara Falls. Canals had been built for centuries, but the Erie Canal was new in almost every aspect. It was the longest at 363 miles, and the rise in terrain from Albany to Buffalo required eighty three locks. The longest level stretch on the entire length was between Lockport and Rochester. With no engineering schools, this project was one of the world's major triumphs, and was called "The Eighth Wonder of the World." The experience learned in the easier areas was the basis for the more difficult feats.

Ground was broken in a field near Rome, NY, on July 4, 1817, and work progressed in both directions. When contracts for the western part were let in 1821, clearing of the woods began in this area, as what is now Middleport was all forest. The canal was opened by sections as work progressed. By 1824 the route was open from Albany to Lockport.

The most difficult and expensive section of the project was the three-mile stretch of twenty-five to thirty-feet deep rock west of Lockport. The second most difficult was through the Montezuma Swamp near Syracuse, where the problem was mosquitoes and epidemics of Swamp Fever. The third most difficult was with the fluid mud in the swamp at Pendleton. The eleven miles of the canal through Tonawanda Creek is the most crooked.

It has often been disputed that "the Irish built the canal," but it was discovered that of all the nationalities that worked on it, the Irish were best suited to the rigors of excavation and more immune to unhealthy conditions. Twelve hundred Irish were employed on the Niagara section. Log barracks and "cook houses" were erected for the single men; a few who brought their wives along erected crude log houses near where they worked.

The old saying that "necessity is the mother of invention" was well demonstrated here in Niagara County. Practically the whole route of our section of the canal had to be cleared of hardwood trees, one of the engineers invented a "stump puller," enabling them to remove thirty to forty stumps a day; cable and winch was produced that could fell a tree of any size. A reward of $100 was offered for a tempered drill hard enough to bore holes into the hard rock to place a gun powder charge for blasting - there was no dynamite at the time. In a short time a young man produced the drill. Another invention was an improved type of wheelbarrow designed for easier emptying of debris. The most important invention was a horse-powered crane that revolutionized excavation work devised by Orange Dibble, an engineer in this area. The cranes, set up every seventy feet, enabled the contractors to finish the canal on time. A Lockport man demonstrated the superiority of cement made from the limestone excavated for the locks, saving the cost of hauling cement from Williamsville.

Even before it was completely finished, a floating library under the sponsorship of E & E Wilcox Encyclopedia of Albany brought the first culture and entertainment to our frontier. The canal was the dividing line between the rough and precarious way of life endured by the early settlers and the beginning of a better life with low cost transportation for getting their products to eastern markets. It also brought eastern products to the frontier.

The official opening of the full length of the "Grand" Erie Canal was on October 26, 1825. The section west of Lockport was finished just the day before! When the flotilla of boats left Buffalo, word was "telegraphed" to New York City by the firing of cannons placed every five to twelve miles apart all along the route. It took about an hour for the message to reach New York. There were cannons at Medina and Knowlesville, and we wonder if there could have been one at Middleport.

This seems like a unique way of announcing to the world that the great undertaking was a success, but this telegraph system had a two-fold purpose. A huge ball was scheduled to be held in New York on opening night, and if anything had happened at Lockport to delay the opening, the ball would also had to have been postponed. Early information was important!

The canal was the first Thruway in the country, although the water in "Clinton's Ditch," as it was referred to by those who opposed the plan, was originally only four feet deep. The only culvert is the one east of Medina. The canal had a monopoly on transportation before the coming of the railroad, and was possibly the most important factor in the opening of the new far Western Territories - Ohio, Indiana, Illinois and Michigan. The total cost was a little over seven million dollars; tolls were first levied in 1820, and by 1836, returns amounted to more than the cost of the project.

C.J. Haines Dry Dock along the southwest side of the canal. This was one of several dry docks according to early maps, all destroyed with the last widening of the canal.
(Image from HTH)

When the first turnpike across the state was built in 1817, an eight-horse freight wagon, with good luck, could make the trip from Albany to Buffalo in fifteen days, charging $100 per ton. Under poor conditions the trip might take six weeks; the canal boat schedule was five to six days, charging six dollars per ton. A freight wagon carried 100 bushels of wheat, or three tons, while the teamster walked;

the same team hitched to a canal boat could haul fifty tons of wheat without great effort. In this area the price of wheat increased from thirty cents to one dollar a bushel. Freight waited at every dock, and towns sprang up overnight.

The early packet boats were thirty to forty feet long and drawn by a three horse tandem, kept at full trot and changed every eight to ten miles, making a speed of about five miles per hour.

Though not from the earliest days of the canal, this photo clearly shows the three horse tandem that walked the towpath pulling the barges. Mules were also used to do this labor for the boat owners.
(Image from RTH)

The canal played a large part in the economy of the community for some time. We know that several of our people owned canal boats during the mid-1800s, carrying grain to New York City and bringing cement back to

Buffalo on the return trip. Warehouses were built on the south side of the canal to house products being shipped, and on the north side, a whole row of dockside stores catered to the needs of the traffic. The stores were open day and night, and dockside drinking water was an accommodation. These stores were destroyed in the widening of the canal 1909-1911.

In the early 1900s, daily packet boats brought people from Medina and Gasport to work at our local canning factory. Mules and horses that pulled the boats were boarded during the winter season at a large barn at the edge of town. For several years, our major employer and manufacturer received the raw material by freight boats, and the heavy "chug" of their engines rattled dish cupboards in houses a quarter-mile away. Bridge tenders were on duty twenty-four hours a day.

Michael E. Carey store on the north bank, one of the many that lined the canal on both sides furnishing the needs of the boaters.
(Image from Wm. Holahan collection)

The Ontario Canning Co., later named the Batavia Preserving Co., was a large employer in Middleport. (Image from MVH)

During the heyday of the canal, the "clang-clang" of the warning bell could be heard any hour of the day or night as the bridge was being raised. After hanging on the Main Street Bridge for fifty years, it was given to the Village by the Department of Transportation when the warning signal lights were installed. With its clapper locked in place, the bell was placed atop a stone "sit upon" in Bell Park Pavilion, the historical mini-park near the bridge approach in 1975.

A large basket manufacturer was located at the canal. Logs were floated down the canal on rafts, and it might be safe to assume that logs arrived at their marina in this manner. The same might be said of the sawmill and lumberyard that were at the east end of the village, on the canal. Our very busy and attractive Basket Factory Restaurant was formerly - the old basket factory, of course!

Enlargements in the 1860s and 1908-1915 brought the canal that we know, from the original 4-foot deep, 40-foot wide, and capable of handling 75-ton barges; to 7-feet deep, 70-feet wide, handling 240-ton barges; and finally 12-deep, 90-feet wide, for 2000-ton barges. The number of locks was decreased from 83 to 72, then to 35. When barges could be used it became the Barge Canal System. It took four years to complete the stretch from Middleport to Lockport, 1909-1912. The "white bridge" across the canal at Vernon Street was taken down and the high bridge was built by erecting retaining walls on either side of the street, north and south of the canal, and filling the space between them on a rising slope to provide a roadbed. With concrete abutments at the ends of each approach, a bridge was thrown across the open span. This was shown on the 1911 village insurance map. The Main Street lift bridge was built in 1914, replacing the 35-year-old Whipple Truss style bridge.

This view is from the north bank of the canal looking east toward the Main Street and Vernon Street bridges. Jackson's Bean House on the right side of the bridge moved to Orchard Street with the widening of the canal. The new bridge is our present lift bridge. This photo is around 1907.
(Image from RTH)

Steam and gasoline engines propelled the huge steel barges, and often these large craft had families onboard. The children played on deck, although during the school year they often stayed ashore with relatives unless they were "home taught." On wash day the laundry would hang on the clothesline; at spring cleaning time the carpets were outside and beaten to remove the dust. On a nice day sometimes the women sat outside to enjoy the sunshine and fresh air. Mules and horses were a thing of the past!

The widening of the canal allowed for larger barges with much larger capacity for goods. This shows one of the larger barges passing under the new lift bridge around 1925.
(Image from RTH)

Commercial traffic on the Barge Canal fell dramatically after the 1959 completion of the St. Lawrence Seaway that allowed ocean-going vessels to pass directly into the Great Lakes.

A great deal of nostalgia is connected with the canal. In recent years the canal has been used primarily by pleasure craft. For probably 40 years or more, in summer our canal bank has been lined with dozens of boats from area Yacht Clubs, particularly over the Labor Day weekend. Electric hookup, picnic tables, lavatories and showers are available for our guests. Receipts in the donation box show their appreciation.

In 1973, the old towpath on the north side of the bank was leveled and re-topped from Lockport to Rochester, making a recreation trail for hikers, joggers and bikers.

The bridge across the canal at Vernon Street was authorized "to be built and maintained at the expense of the State and included in the Erie Canal enlargement program." The bridge was closed by the state in 1991, declaring it to be unsafe; it was taken down in 1997. A ten-inch water line supplying the north part of the village was carried along the side of the bridge, and was relocated under the canal in the state project.

The ground was leveled on both sides of the canal, and "Margaret Droman Park" was created on the north side, named for our Village Clerk who had served for 30 years. Information kiosks were placed at the park and at the canal bridge at Gasport.

Dedication of the old tower bell next to the canal on June 6, 1975, by Mayor Lawrence Krolak. (Image from MVH)

View of the pavilion dedicated at Margaret Droman Park in honor of her long and faithful service as Middleport Village Clerk-Treasurer. (Image from MVH)

Early Middleport

The earliest item that we have seen in print mentioning Middleport was from the diary of Asa Fitch, who, with a group of founders of what is now Rensselaer Polytechnic Institute, was traveling the canal for the purpose of collecting specimens of natural history.

On Wednesday, May 17, 1826, the party spent the night at Middleport. The journal reported that "at Middleport the buildings are chiefly of logs, a bit grotesque but not uninteresting. However, happiness might dwell here." Also "the new hotel nearing completion will be one of the finest in the area." This would have been a hotel at the present location of the Credit Union, probably the Pierce Hotel.

William Taylor sold land to Rev. John Copeland in 1827, giving a warranty deed to the trustees of the Methodist Episcopal Church. The church was built right away, on the south side of Park Avenue near Main Street. The first school in the village was the small brick academy built across the street from the church that opened in January 1842.

In 1830 John Macker was the first tailor here, followed by Bridgeman, Stone & Snell, and Charles Wilcox.

VanBrocklin's stone building on Vernon near State Street was originally used as a blast furnace but has housed a variety of businesses over the years. (Image from Wm. Holahan collection)

The stone building at the corner of Vernon and State Streets was built by John VanBrocklin in 1840, the first and only blast furnace in the village, and operated until at least 1860. The building has been used pretty continuously by a variety of businesses: a bicycle shop, a blacksmith, a theater, temporary school classrooms, and several light manufacturing businesses.

And at this time, we first heard of our Brass Band that went through several names and periods of activity for sixty years.

The Village cemetery was bounded on the west by Maple Avenue and on the south by the railroad, consisting of four acres. The Middleport Burial Association was incorporated in 1841 and was used for about seventy years. When burials were no longer being made and there were no funds for upkeep, and because of the growth of the village and the proximity of new housing, it was declared a danger to public health and was legally disbanded in 1915. A commission of six citizens was granted title to the property for the purpose of exhuming and removing the remains, and reinterment. The costs were paid from the sale of the property. The graves were moved to cemeteries of any living families' choice; otherwise, the stones were reset in rows on the west side of LeValley Cemetery, Pearson Road.

The railroad came to Middleport in 1852, and with it and the canal for transportation, we became a large shipping center. In the 1870s, newspapers reported of fruit being shipped from the canal villages. In 1873, Middleport showed 12,000 barrels of winter fruit to be shipped to New York, Eastern markets paying $3.00/barrel. A large export trade to England began an important outlet for part of the apple crop. Queen Victoria demanded Niagara County apples for the royal table.

Middleport train depot on Vernon Street with hotel wagon waiting to transport travelers.
(Image from MVH)

The Village of Middleport was incorporated on March 28, 1859, but not without considerable dissention and bitter words. The poorer opposed increasing taxes and accused the more well-to-do of dishonesty and evil doings; a counter charge was of blind selfishness. It took many years for the hard feelings to be overcome. The first elected trustees were: A. J. Baker, Buel F. Barnes, Horace Pierce, Thomas F. Smith and Francis L. Taylor. Taylor was chosen president, and Peter B. Knower, village clerk. One of the first ordinances passed concerned "restraining cattle, horses, sheep, swine and geese from running at large." The population was 689 people.

Looking south on Main Street at the young and bustling town of Middleport.
(Image from MVH)

A Lockport newspaper reported that "our young sister, Middleport, we notice has very many attractive features for one so young," citing a fine public school, three or four churches, grocery and dry goods stores, and a fine hotel. "We do not see why Middleportians should not be happy." Another publication said that "when the community had grown to the dignity of a village, it was referred to by jealous rivals as 'mud port'" - possibly because of the condition of the streets after a rain.

On the 1860 village map, the streets north of the canal are the same as they are today. There were no streets off State Street; Church Street ended at the creek; Vernon Street extended south of the railroad only to South Street.

The part of the village north of the center line of Sherman Street lies in the Town of Hartland.

Wildcat Creek

The growth of Middleport has been attributed to the canal and the railroad, but many years ago, Elmer A. Vary, then our native senior citizen, felt that a great deal of credit should be given to Jeddo Creek, or as it was called then, "Wildcat Creek." In the late 1800s, the creek supplied employment for more than 400 people in the several manufacturing firms that used water in their work, or were powered by steam, water wheel or both. Passing through the village, the creek flowed into four ponds that were a fisherman's paradise in which all kinds of fish were caught. At one time the creek flowed all year around.

Wildcat Creek rushing through town around 1915
(Image from MVH)

Before the village water works dam was constructed south of the village, at the time of heavy rains, the creek would cause flash flooding. Water rushed over the road on Route 31, washing out wooden bridges as it flowed north, flooding the streets and forming a good-sized lake just south of the railroad. At spring thaw, dynamiting was necessary to clear the ice cake jams from the culvert under the railroad. New York Central became alarmed about the pressure against the roadbed, and in about 1915 they enlarged the culvert.

Starting south of the village on the Ernest Freeman farm, near the creek was the barn (used as a machine shop) where Freeman invented and patented in 1904 a high-pressure spray rig that won first prize at the Chicago World's Fair. This business was the stepping-stone of the Niagara Sprayer Company, now FMC.

Ernest Freeman with his award winning spraying rig and the beginning of the Niagara Sprayer Company. (Image from MVH)

Downstream at what is now Greg's Tractor Repair, the stream ran close by the R. T. Chase Cheese factory, which was powered by a steam engine and a steam boiler. In the "Jottings by the Wayside" column by Moses Richardson, he told of tricking each of the merchants in Middleport into giving him a large slice of cheese to "sample" by asking about the flavor. In 1872 he wrote that 130 cows furnished milk for 400 pounds of cheese per day. This later became the Chase & Son Feed Mill.

Just north of the mill was a two-story cooper shop owned by Elbert Smith, where water from the creek was pumped into large wooden tanks to soak the wooden strips that were made into barrel hoops.

On the west bank of the creek, south of the railroad, was the machine shop of inventor Edgar Knapp, who patented and manufactured the very successful Knapp Giant Bean Picker, used to clean and sort beans for market from about 1890 until he sold it in the early 1900s. North of the tracks on Main Street was the Compton & Bennett Cold Storage. Next to it the lumberyard of Tom Jackson was on both sides of the creek. Whenever a flash flood hit, men from the yard had to go downstream to fish out the lumber that had floated away.

Edgar Knapp's Giant Bean Picker, used to clean and
sort beans for market.
(Image from MVH)

At the corner of Orchard and Church Streets, for
some time, there was a broom factory. Another inventor, E.
L. Downey, M.D., took over the broom factory and bottled a
liquid insecticide called "Downside," and in 1904
advertised that it didn't smell like rotten eggs like that of his
competitor. He outgrew the building and built a small two-
story plant east of the Resseugie, later Rhinehart, mill on
Kelly Avenue at the railroad.

"Downside" was put up in glass bottles with an
interesting system for filling them. The bottles were stood
upright in metal washtubs and covered with a wire mesh to
prevent them from floating. Pails of "Downside" were
poured over the bottles until they were full; a faucet at the

bottom of the tub drained off the surplus. A stick was pushed into the bottle, displacing enough of the liquid so that the corks could be inserted.

Just north of the Orchard Street bridge, the first pond backed up under the bridge and behind the houses on Orchard Street, although except for the creek bed, it has been filled in for many years. On the northeast corner of this pond a raceway ran to a water wheel that operated the Buel Barnes flour mill on the north bank of the canal. No water was taken from the canal as it all came from this pond. The mill burned in 1858, leaving only the bare stone walls standing. It was rebuilt in 1883 as the Ontario Preserving Company. Monroe Woodworth's stave mill, powered by a steam engine, was also on the east side of the pond, facing the south bank of the canal.

Monroe Woodworth's stave mill was along the southwest side of the canal and produced barrels to transport liquids or dry goods. The water from Wildcat Creek powered their steam engines.
(Image from Mary B. Davenport)

On the west side of the pond were the two dry docks where canal boats were built and repaired. West of the dock, a bay opened directly into the canal so that the boats could be floated into the docks.

A boat in dry dock near the spillway on Church Street. (Image from Wm. Holahan collection)

The next pond downstream was the grist mill pond, extending along North Hartland from Mechanic Street to the four-story stone flour mill at the corner of Sherman Road. The pond was about square in shape and a waterfall flooded the area that became Trail Home Estates Park in 1958. On the southwest corner the Carey Brothers Ice House stored twelve to fourteen inch-thick blocks of ice cut from the pond. On the east side of the pond a small culvert ran under Hartland Street to a small pond on the Gould Greenhouse property supplying them with water.

Carey's Ice House harvested ice in the winter that would be stored and used in family ice boxes throughout the year. The ice house burned in 1930s, but by then, other means of producing ice had been invented and were used by cold storage facilities.
(Image from a Buffalo, NY newspaper around 1910)

The paper millpond extended pretty much from Sherman Road to Chase Road along Hartland Street. At the southwest corner at Chase Road was the Sterritt Paper Mill, again powered by a water wheel and a steam engine. It operated on two twelve-hour shifts per day; bales of waste paper were received by canal and rail. The mill was destroyed by fire in 1904.

Downstream a short way was the dam that threw water into a raceway running north to the heading mill and machine shop on the northeast corner of the next pond. George Smith was an inventor who patented and manufactured barrel tools, hoop bending machines and a machine that would finish both ends of a barrel at the same time. He also had a cooper shop on the canal where he built a very tight, smooth barrel, used by Mr. Barnes for shipping flour. The barrels had rack hoops that locked together without nails.

At the northwest of the heading mill pond was the Sterritt Heading Mill that was taken over by the Middleport Electric Company about 1903 and furnished the village with its first electric arc street lights. This plant was powered by a water wheel and a steam engine.

Mr. Elmer Vary recalled that this beautiful stream of water and the four waterfalls with rapids between the ponds made a beautiful picture. The natural beauty, in the abundance of reeds, colorful aquatic plants, variety of water birds, the busy muskrat, and the evening bullfrog concerts late into the night were not to be forgotten.

When bushel baskets and other small containers took over the shipping market, the stave yards, heading mills and cooper shops faded out of the picture. Many years ago, there were several saw mills along the creek.

In 1902, a flash flood washed out the north bank of all the ponds, and they were never fully replaced. In the early 1930s, the upper grist mill pond was filled for swimming and ice skating and was a very popular spot for a short time. About that time the paper mill pond was restocked with fish. There is practically no evidence of these ponds today.

The 1800s

Several people in Middleport owned canal boats in the early 1860s: Benjamin S. Day, George W. King, Milo E. McKee, J. P. Niles, Chardon Pettis and Alfred Southwick. Chauncey A. Niles owned two boats: "Compton & O'Dell" and "L. H. Spaulding," (both names of Middleport merchants), carrying wheat to New York City and bringing cement back to Buffalo.

On April 28, 1863, the completion of the Cady & Dunton Dry Docks for the building and repairing of boats was important to the village. The docks consisted of one double and one single lock. After the water had been let in, the canaler "Ray Delano" of Capt. Chauncey Niles was the first to enter the dock. Next came the "John B. Weld" of Capt. Benjamin S. Day, and last "Urbin C. Thurston" of Capt. Loomis went into the single lock. The Middleport Band and the presence of about 200 citizens made for a festive dedication, after which dinner was served at the Pierce Hotel, the location of the present Credit Union. The Dry Dock was destroyed in the widening of the canal 1908-1912.

*The office of Hiram Robertson's lumber company at the
end of Robertson Street.
(Image from Wm. Holahan collection)*

Mr. Hiram A. Robertson deserves a great deal of credit for the early growth of Middleport. In 1860 he began to develop the fifty-acre tract of land that his father had purchased thirty years earlier. He laid out Maple Avenue and all the streets from Vernon Street east between State Street and the canal. He placed trees along the streets and erected a large number of houses. He was an entrepreneur with several small businesses before founding the Robertson Lumber Company at the end of Robertson Street. He and George Cheshire had a cabinet making and coffin business in the building that they erected on Front Street in 1870 that is still there. His son-in-law, and then his granddaughter, continued the lumber business until 1959, when it was sold to Clifford Schnackel and Stanley D. McDonald, becoming the Middleport Lumber Company.

Mr. Robertson married Helen M. Parker of Lockport and New York City. Parker entered Hahneman Medical College in Chicago at the age of fifty, graduating with honors in 1889. Our first female doctor, she practiced medicine at the family home, 33 State Street, for thirty-five years until shortly before her death.

Helen Parker Robertson, wife of Hiram Robertson,
Middleport's first female physician.
(Image from MVH)

The Underground Railroad had been active for many years before slavery was abolished by the outcome of the Civil War. The locations of the Underground Railroad stations cannot be verified, as people didn't keep records of events that could prove them to be breaking the law or reveal routes taken by the runaway slaves. But for as long as I can remember, the old Freeman house, recently the Shops at Teapot Hollow on Route 31, and the old Odell place, now the Ortman farm on Griswold Street I were said to have been such stops.

The Bob Durdans family who lived in the Freeman house for many years, were sure that the slaves were directed to the trap door in the woodshed leading to a root cellar. A passageway led to the four-foot-high crawl space under the main house to the flagstone-based porches at the front and east side doors of the house. Wood slat flooring provided plenty of air circulation and the flagstones assured secrecy. The hiding places undoubtedly were built in by Mr. Sawtell who built the house in the late 1820s. The porches had ample space to harbor ten people. The dormer roof over the east porch was also used, but how anyone gained access was a mystery.

One of the specifications of permission to use a hideout was that the family not be aware of the transients. The cook was apparently allowed to provide food, as metal eating utensils were found in all three areas that were ingenious in both their obviousness and inaccessibility. Newspapers dated prior to the 1850s were found in the porch; a publication at the Letchworth State Park Museum told of an unsuccessful slave hunt in the area. Slave trackers followed the group to Batavia, then to Griswold Street at Middleport where they disappeared, leaving no further trail.

Serious fires were a way of life in the earlier days. In 1876 a fire on the west side of Main Street destroyed the Compton Opera House, now 26 Main Street. On November 28, 1878, fire broke out on the east side of Main Street, spreading from house to store. A telegram was sent to

Lockport requesting help from their fire department. Their equipment was loaded on a work train, and within an hour three fire companies arrived at Middleport. The train made a remarkable time of fourteen minutes for the twelve-mile trip. However, by 5:00 pm all eighteen buildings were gone. The stores were rebuilt, and burned again on January 23, 1879. In March, John Lennon of Lockport contracted to build the present brick stores "as soon as the weather permits," and by October 1st they were completed.

The west side . . .

. . . and the east side of Main Street showing the old wooden buildings that were destroyed in the disastrous fires of 1876 and 1878. Insurance companies insisted that the new buildings to be constructed be made of brick. (Images from Wm. Holahan collection)

While drilling for a well on the Nearing property on Francis Street in 1887, gas was struck at twenty-five feet. "It was lighted several times and burned quite brilliantly," starting talk of forming a stock company to supply the village with gas. Several years before, gas was struck, again on Francis Street on the Schlager property.

When bicycling reached its peak in 1897, a cinder "side path" was laid out along the west side of Stone Road for the "wheelmen," with an arched entrance at Sleeper Street. The path continued east along the Ridge Road to Lyndonville; there was also a side path south of the village. At times they were Deputy Sheriff patrolled, and anyone riding without a tag was arrested. The fine was $5, which seems like the "severe penalty," as promised.

In 1899 the Middleport Power Company was formed and started the first electric power here, though it met with little success. The Middleport Gas & Electric Company was formed in 1901.

Things were becoming a bit more modern and the new century was welcomed in with a big street parade at midnight December 31, 1901, at the end of the 19th century. From an old newspaper article:

"The Twentieth Century was ushered in by our citizens at midnight Monday in a blaze of fireworks, booming of cannon, ringing of church bells, blowing of whistles, and general bedlam reigned supreme for a short period."

The parade formed at the fire building and was headed by the Middleport Cornet Band. Next came the float representing a house in which there sat an old woman, holding an infant, symbolic of the new century; following thereafter came the general participants dressed in grotesque costumes. Those in procession were well supplied with fire-works.

The parade moved exactly at midnight, and passed over the following streets: Main, South Vernon, State and Main, to the fire building. Red fire was burned on every corner, and the Roman candles illuminated the heavens.

The celebration was a success in every respect and everyone was satisfied. The century had been ushered in with a "hurrah"; in case anyone has an idea they could improve on the celebration of Monday evening, the opportunity is theirs at the dawn of the 21st Century, but we are quite satisfied with the present one. Apparently, everyone was satisfied!

Into The New Century

Middleport will be heard of as far away as the Arctic Circle, for early in the New Year the Canning Factory shipped 150 dozen one-pound cans of jelly to New York City to be placed on a vessel that will sail with the Expedition to the North Pole.

The Bell Telephone Company began removing cranks from their telephones as a new invention permits calling Central by lifting the receiver.

As part of the Town of Royalton for forty to fifty years, the village felt that the only benefit they received was an opportunity to vote for the highway commissioner and to pay over $50,000 as their share of the Town of Royalton tax. In 1907 the trustees appointed village president Dr. E. L. Downey and attorney George F. Thompson to go to Albany to have a bill introduced, for the second time, that would revive an attempt to separate from the Town of Royalton. The southern half to be "Royalton," and the northern half to be "Watson," in honor of life-long citizen Israel M. Watson. Apparently the attempt was not a success this time, either.

The Buffalo-Lockport-Rochester Railway began operation November 17, 1908, entered the village at the corner of Alfred Street and Park Avenue, along Park Avenue and Church Streets, and out at Watson Avenue, and across St. Stephen's Cemetery.

The trolley car turning from Church across Main Street and down to Park Ave.
(Image from the RHCL)

Also, the police officers were trying to rid the village of tramps who were constantly asking for food, making life miserable for the women.

Theodore Dosch, manager of the Niagara Sprayer Company, and attorney George Sheldon found the springs on the high ground south of the village that led to the development of the Middleport Water Company in 1911.

The RMS Titanic sank off Cape Rose, Newfoundland in 1912, and among those lost was twenty-four-year-old William B. Alexander, who was on his way to Middleport to make a surprise visit to his sister, Gertrude Alexander Jex, who lived at 97 Main Street.

A.D.Rich Hook and Ladder Co. in front of the Hotel Rich on Main Street. This was one of the three early fire companies that would later merge to form the Middleport Fire Dept. (Image from MVH)

The Middleport Fire Department was organized in 1922. Later that year the hobby of several residents was to listen to European radio stations who alternately broadcast for an hour, then were silent for an hour to receive from the United States. With the speed limit recently having been raised from fifteen to twenty miles per hour, in April 1924, George Mufford began duty as traffic policeman. He was furnished with a regulation uniform and a Harley-Davidson motorcycle speedy enough to protect the citizens from cars racing through the streets. The first person to be apprehended was Medina attorney Irving L'Hommedieu who was hurrying to the Court House in Albion when he passed the school doing 42 mph. He was very repentant, and Judge Seaman gave him a reasonably light fine.

The high school students had the pleasure of seeing a film produced by Niagara Sprayer Company, "Turning Dust Into Dollars," which was amusing to them as so many of the "actors" were local people.

We have copies of four pieces of sheet music written by Elma R. Whited of 17 Park Avenue in 1928. She wrote the words and music to "Oh Light Of My Life," "Mother How Sweet The Name," and "Oh So Lovely," a fox trot; Prof. E. Wunderlich composed the music for her "Sweet Victory Of Love."

OH, LIGHT OF MY LIFE

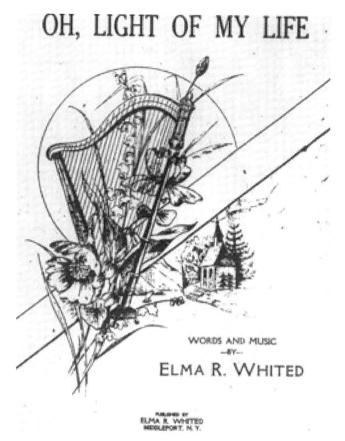

WORDS AND MUSIC
—BY—
ELMA R. WHITED

PUBLISHED BY
ELMA R. WHITED
MIDDLEPORT, N. Y.

Elma R. Whited, resident of Park Avenue and wife of the local undertaker, created several pieces of music during the 1920s.
(Image from MVH)

In 1934, the poplar trees in the village were ordered to be cut as the roots ran into the sewers and water mains. The wood was given to needy families.

At the end of 1938, Middleport and Gasport were getting the fancy new dial telephones.

And we can't go past 1941 without remembering December 7th, "the day that will live in infamy," the day that changed all" of our lives, and changed the world as it had been known.

The mayor had been proposing for two years that the village office be staffed and open during business hours. In 1942, he resigned because of the lax manner in which the Board had worked. With a budget in excess of $40,000 they only had the office open during tax collecting days and, the village clerk was seldom there.

In 1950 the seventh annual employee and family picnic of Niagara Chemical Division, FMC, was held at the Rod & Gun Club grounds. Well over 700 attended and many of the older employees said that it was by far the finest picnic ever. The food was plentiful with 1700 hot dogs and rolls, 1920 bottles of pop, sixty gallons of ice cream, seventy gallons of clam broth and twenty halves of beer. At 5:30 the chow line began: sweet potatoes, sweet corn, 720 lobster tails, 720 halves of chicken, and 4000 clams.

Annual clambakes were popular with the employees of Niagara Sprayer throughout the years. Many pictures exist with the annual gathering of employees throughout Niagara County. This one is dated 1938. (Image from MVH)

The Rotary Club had sponsored Middleport Boy Scout Troop #23 for many years, but finding a meeting place was always a problem. The barn on the former William Ewing property showed promise, and with the cooperation of owners Mr. and Mrs. Christoph Poehlman, the club purchased the entire eighteen acre tract on Route 31 known as "Rocky," in 1951. The area had for a long time been a popular spot for the children and youth of the community, and the acreage would provide ideal Scouting grounds, and it was hoped that other youth organizations might use the building.

The completion of the $2 million FMC Research Center off Vernon Street at the end of 1963 was the greatest single step forward in the evolution of Niagara Chemical from its humble beginning in 1904.

In the summer of 1967, a partial state of emergency was lifted after 2 days of trying to find the source of a suspected gasoline leak into the village sewer system. Mr. Raduns of 8 Church Street was burned after a minor explosion in his basement, and a "pressure buildup" on Church Street blew a manhole cover from its position.

The Niagara County and New York State District Civil Defense Directors were working with the Middleport village officials and fire department to locate the source of the leak affecting Main Street from Route 31 to Church, Church Street to S. Hartland and all of S. Hartland. All tests came up negative.

The owner of the Sunoco Station at Main Street & Route 31, L. S. Freeman, discovered a gas shortage in one of his three underground tanks by periodic stick-depth checks. The tanks were pumped out and flooded with water, and were abandoned.

The fire-damaged Niagara Sprayer sulphur warehouse behind the Main Street stores alongside the canal, was purchased by the village and was rebuilt by the Department of Public Works employees to house an office, machine shop and a garage for their equipment. It was ready for use by January 1972.

Four small stores on Main Street were demolished by S & C Corporation of Barker in anticipation of building a covered mall around a courtyard to adjoin the Peterson Drug Store that fronted on Vernon Street. Re-development came to a dead end because tenants had not been attracted. The area became the well-used parking lot.

The Lockport paper ran an article about the demolition of these stores on the east side of Main Street in July of 1972. The dream of new stores never materialized and the area remains an empty parking lot to this day. (Image from Lockport Union Sun and Journal)

In 1972, the Girl Scout glass recycling project got off to a slow start in the fall, but a gift of 16,000 cases of obsolete thirty-two ounce bottles by the RJR Food Inc., Lockport, brought a flurry of activity. The immense undertaking brought cooperation from various organizations and individuals and from the village and employees in crushing the glass and transferring it to the buyer at Brockport.

The village office space had been very cramped for a long time and in early 1974, work began to renovate the village building that had housed the fire trucks. The increased floor space provided for a larger office, a much needed conference room, and a fire-proof vault. The project was unique in that for the most part the project was an internal undertaking. A great deal of the work was done by Arthur Kraatz, Superintendent. of Public Works, and his men during what would normally be a slow season. Mayor Krolak, a cabinet maker and builder by trade lent his expertise. The outside hire was mason George Grapes, Sr., who came out of retirement to do the brick facing on the front of the building, retaining the period style of the downtown section. The small, adjoining former village office became the new police office.

The new Village Hall in the site of the old fire truck building. Notice the Star Theater building is still in place but soon to be demolished because of high renovation costs. (Image from MVH)

At the end of the year a public open house celebrated the new facility, and the village office moved into their new quarters on January 1st.

A move had been under way for some time to renovate the old Star Theater next door for use as a community center. Renovation costs were going to be prohibitive and it was decided to demolish the building.

The Star Theater on Main Street
(Image from RTH)

In recognition of Bicentennial celebrations in 1976, four markers were dedicated with a brief description on each one: the first home of early settler Asher Freeman, the canal towpath opened in 1824, the Phillip Freeman home reputed to be a stop on the Underground Railroad, and the Universalist Church built in 1841.

As one enters the village signs with our logo have been greeting visitors for 30 years: "Middleport A Friendly Community ," and a canal boat, the result of a logo contest.

Village sign with logo can be found on the main roads leading into the village.
(Image from MVH)

Perfect weather was on hand on June 3, 1979, for the Rotary Club sponsored dedication ceremony of the Community Building, known over the years as the "Scout House." About $30,000 from various sources had been put into the project, and over 400 people toured the building and its handsome new kitchen, a new "west wing" addition, rest room facilities, and picnic and play area. Rotary was in the beginning stage of a five-year project that, when completed, would see a pavilion, horseshoe courts and a children's playground.

The new Scout House ready for its Rotary dedication on June 3, 1979. This facility is still used today for many community activities.
(Image from the Medina Journal Register)

On Sunday afternoon, November 11th, 1979, Main and State Streets were blocked off as time turned back to the early 1900s when the Catholic Diocese of Buffalo was putting together a movie, "Tuck Everlasting" based on the children's story by Natalie Babbitt.

These streets were chosen for this segment of the movie because of the still "old look" of the brick buildings, with the windows and store signs covered. Lawrence Steimer of Gasport took part with his horse drawn trap-style carriage, and filming was done from the back of a pickup truck which crew members pushed down the street for the appearance of movement. The movie was shown on Channel 4 Buffalo the following year.

Middleport's fine old buildings were the perfect background for the filming of the movie "Tuck Everlasting" based on the book by Natalie Babbit. Several locals had walk on roles in the movie.
(Image from the Medina Journal Register)

In 1982, the village had 600 homes housing 329 dogs, leading to a leash law.

The village was a beehive of activity on June 18, 1986, when the United States Postal Department held the First Day Issue Ceremony for the green and white, 17¢ Belva Lockwood stamp; part of the Great American Series, honoring the Town of Royalton native for her many achievements. A pioneer for women's rights, she founded the first co-educational school in Washington, D.C., and was the first woman to be nominated for president in 1884, running again in 1888.

The Royalton Hartland Central School auditorium was filled to a standing-room-only crowd of at least 900 people. Presiding was the General Manager of the Buffalo Division, United States Postal Service; introduction of distinguished guests and remarks by Norma Z. Wollenberg, chairman of the Belva Ann Lockwood stamp committee, Town of Royalton Historical Society, and address by Roger P. Craig, Assistant. Postmaster General. Honored guests were Christopher Calle, designer of the stamp, the postmasters of the Middleport and Gasport post offices, and the president of the Town of Royalton Historical Society. Following the ceremony a reception was held in the Royalton Hartland Central School Elementary School gymnasium.

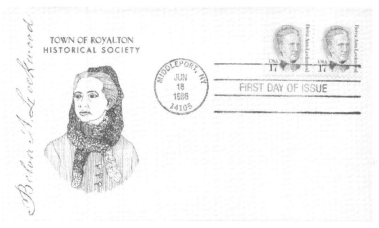

The US Postal Service honored Belva Lockwood, first woman to be nominated for president of the US back in 1884 and 1888, long before women had the right to vote. A ceremony at the Royalton Hartland High School unveiled the beautiful stamp to commemorate this very special day.
(Image from MVH)

In 1993 the Carmen Road canal bridge was removed, to be replaced by a new span.

The rebuilding of the Carmen Road canal bridge, photographed by a local resident on his daily walks. (Image by Tom Sheldon)

A program designed to encourage communities to take a serious interest in the care of their trees was started in 1994 by Robert Querns and Richard Pease of the Rotary Club. Four of the National Arbor Day Foundation's standards have to be met: establishing a tree board, a tree care ordinance, a community forestry program, and an Arbor Day observance. Middleport has received recognition as a "Tree City USA" by the National Arbor Day Foundation, having honored its commitment to community forestry. The trees in the village have been surveyed by Michael Tree and Landscape Consultants of Ontario, NY.

The summer of 1996 was exciting for Middleport: Village native "Lou" Rosselli and a Roy-Hart wrestler, compiling a high school career record of 156-8, earned a spot on the United States Olympic Wrestling Team. And on the way he became a two-time New York State Champion, a three-Time National Collegiate Champion from Edinboro University, as well as an Academic All-American.

Lou Rosselli, Roy Hart graduate and wrestler representing the USA in the 1996 Olympic Games in Atlanta.
(Image from MVH)

The Olympic flame was lit in Athens in March before arriving in Los Angeles. From there it began an eighty-four-day, 15,000-mile parade through the United States, passing through thousands of communities in forty-two states. A caravan of about thirty trucks, autos, motorcycles, and bicycles, led by the Georgia State Police, carried the flame.

From Lockport the motorcade carrying the Olympic Flame made its way down Route 31 on June 12th, and people lined the road to greet their "once in a lifetime" glimpse of the flame as it made its way on to Atlanta.

Business and many homes displayed banners expressing their pride and good wishes for Lou in his quest for an Olympic medal.
(Image from MVH)

July 11th was proclaimed "Lou Rosselli Day," a large banner across Main Street read "Going for the Gold: Wrestling Olympian Lou Rosselli, Atlanta, 1996." In the evening about 200 friends and well-wishers assembled in front of the village hall. Here Mayor Piedmont presented a proclamation, Dan Seaman presented a proclamation on behalf of his brother Assemblyman David Seaman, and the post office gave Rosselli a framed series of Commemorative Olympic Stamps. He autographed T-shirts and refreshments followed.

All around the Middleport area, business signs displayed "Go Lou!" and "Bring it home, Lou!" and "Go for the Gold!" His family said that despite all the attention, he remains a modest, small-town kid" He didn't understand what all the fuss was about because he'd been wrestling internationally since high school.

In the third Olympic match, in the 114.5 pound weight class, he suffered an elbow broken in two places. After the allowed time-out he was able to finish the match - and win it!, even though that arm was useless. It was the first time that he had been injured in competition. He had to withdraw from further competition, and needless to say that it was VERY disappointing for him, and also for us at home! He retired from actively competing in 2000. He went on to become assistant wrestling coach at Ohio State.

The three days of activity over Labor Day weekend 1997, for the first time in over twenty years, began on Saturday morning. Events included a small midway, a kiddie parade, a breakfast, an auction, miscellaneous food vendors, several dinners, musical entertainment and a "Battle of the Bands." Fireworks were set off on the grounds of the Royalton Hartland Elementary School. It was a drink and drug free family event coordinated by Joyce Bateman, director of the Community Youth Center, in celebration of their tenth anniversary. The Universalist Church parsonage next to the church, vacant for some time, was made available as the center for as long as it remained in operation. Renovations were made by donated services and materials; volunteer staffing and annual fund drives made it a reality.

Village Clerk Margaret Droman retired having served the village for thirty-five years, receiving an award from the New York State Conference of Mayors.

Village Clerk Treasurer, Margaret Droman busy at work in the village hall offices in 1974.
(Image from MVH)

Another New Century

At the beginning of the 21st Century, we all survived the Y2K scare as computers read "00" correctly as "2000" and not "1900" as has been feared. Airplanes continued to fly on schedule, public utilities served as usual, and computers operated smoothly.

Tied together by satellite television, the world's 200 countries and their twenty-four time zones became a showcase of cultures, welcoming each time zone as it entered 2000.

Julia Maedl was elected to the Village Board as the second woman Trustee in 1992, and was appointed Deputy Mayor in 1996. In 2001 "Julie" was elected our first woman Mayor. Nancy Walker was the first woman trustee in 1987 but had to resign when she moved from the area.

Julie Maedl, first female mayor of the village, serving from 2001 – 2011.

When Middleport awakened on September 11, 2001, it was just another peaceful Tuesday morning, but that was to be short-lived. At 8:48am a plane had crashed into the north tower of the World Trade Center, New York City, and we all assumed that it was an accident. But just after 9:00, when another plane hit the south tower, all who were watching it on television had a feeling of terror. THAT was NO accident!! We wouldn't realize what had happened until hours later when we learned that a terrorist group had overtaken the flight crews and turned the planes toward the New York skyline. Another day that will live in infamy.

*After the attacks on 9/11, "God Bless America" became
the most spoken phrase in our country and village and
homes were decorated with the American flag and
buntings of red, white and blue.
(Image from MVH)*

The Middleport Community Choir, with members
from the Lutheran, Methodist, Roman Catholic and
Universalist churches, was scheduled to leave the following
day for a two-week once-in-a-lifetime concert travel trip to
Lübbecke, Germany. Immediately all plans were put on
hold. For several days there was much indecision about their
future plans before they were cancelled. Pastor Pollock and
Father Badding were going with the choir and were in the
midst of all the confusion.

Alone, Rev. Triplett hurriedly put together a
wonderful community prayer service at 7:00pm on the 12th,
with all the local pastors and several laypeople participating.
Prayers, scriptures, patriotic readings, faith-hymns, and a

heart-felt rendition of "Love Grows Here" by the choir, made for a soul-stirring program.

The choir had put on a bon voyage concert at St. Stephen's previously and having practiced for the tour for two years, they wanted to put the time spent to good use. On the 16th they put on another concert for the benefit of the Red Cross, and they raised $2000. They also put on benefits during October and November at Medina, Gasport and Lockport. Especially during that first year, small American flags were used so much in flower beds and on autos.

On September 11, 2002, an outdoor memorial service was held at the Bates, Wallace & Heath Funeral Home in front of a four foot by twenty-four foot wide memorial wall displaying the names of all the 3044 persons known to have perished at the World Trade Center, the Pentagon and with Flight #93 that crashed in a field in Pennsylvania. Beginning with September 1st, the Funeral Home released 3044 environmentally-friendly latex balloons, a few each day. The memorial walls were installed at the 100 Key Memories-affiliated locations across the country.

This memorial wall was erected on the lawn of the Bates, Wallace and Heath Funeral Home in tribute to those who died in the attacks of September 11, 2001. (Image from MVH)

A chair lift to the second floor at the village hall was brought about through the efforts of Joyce Bateman, for the benefit of the American Legion members.

A contract went into effect with the Town of Royalton for Middleport police to furnish speed enforcement in specific areas of the Town. There is always an officer on duty in the village whenever one is on duty in the Town.

Restored McLintock Loomis clock hanging outside the Village Hall.
(Image from MVH)

A restored circa 1910 McClintock Loomis clock known as the Middleport Community Clock has graced the second story of the village hall since 2004. Saved from the wrecking ball in the 1960s, it had been a permanent fixture hanging from the corner of the Fenton Hotel. Through the efforts of the Tourism Committee and the Barge Canal Art Center, the "Time for Middleport" project raised $20,000 in less than two years. Illuminated at night, this piece of history brings a touch of nostalgia to the village.

*Mural on the State Street side of the building created by
Stacey Kirby.
(Image from MVH)*

During 2007, a twelve foot by 16 foot acrylic mural
on the State Street side of the former brick drug store
building was done from a canal scene photo by David
Stockton. Flanked on either side by older scenes of the
village, all scenes were trimmed with gold frame borders
and topped with the motto, "Middleport, NY: a friendly
community." The painting was done by artisan Stacey
Kirby, and was sponsored by the Barge Canal Art Center
and the Tourism Committee providing extra funding. It is
planned to be the first in a series.

In the fall of 2007, our little village of 1917 residents
was named by Business Week Magazine, working with

national real estate researcher Onboard, as the 11th of 50 places in the country listed, as a "great place to raise children," having the right combination of safety, community and education. The criteria were test scores, cost of living, recreational and cultural activities, number of schools and risk of crime. As Mayor Maedl said, "it won't affect anything major, but it is good news."

Business Week Magazine named Middleport 11th out of 50 best places to raise children in this country. (Image from MVH)

The Common

On the 1860 map of the Village, the first after incorporation, the area between Main Street and Vernon Street, now the park, was "Common Hall." Possibly our development was similar to the old New England villages, where the public buildings surrounded the village square, in that in 1827 the Methodist Episcopal Church was built on the southwest corner of the Common; in 1841, the Universalist Church was erected on Main Street at the end of the Common, and in 1843 the Academy was built across from the Methodist Episcopal Church.

The Common ran between Vernon and Main Street and was filled with trees planted in the 1800s. (Image from the RHCL)

At the southeast end of the Common, District #1 school was built in 1846 with the second addition by 1898; across the corner the Vernon Hotel was erected by 1874, becoming the Grove House by 1886, and burned nine years later. The new Methodist Episcopal Church was built on the site in 1899. In 1889 the Presbyterian Church was built at the east end of the Common on Vernon Street.

Trees on either side of the park were planted 1878-1884.

The coming of the trolley in 1908 created a furor as the route was planned to come down Liberty Street, across the park, and out Church Street. After litigation, the tracks did go through the park, and possibly to appease those who were opposed, the whole street was named Park Avenue. It officially became a street in 1915; curbing was laid in the early 1920s.

The original buildings in the park burned: the Grove House in 1896, the old church and the school in 1910, and the old "Common" became a park. $1000 was received from the estate of Truman Jennings, mayor of the village 1917-1921, for a fountain to be placed in the park. The next year, a $500 Memorial was received from the wife of R. S. Hawkins, village clerk 1907-1910, to beautify the park.

In 1930, a pond was put in near the southeast end of Park Avenue to surround the memorial fountain, and the addition of shrubbery and benches created a small park that became a popular spot for the citizenry to relax and "watch the world go by." The fountain statue chosen for the pond was Berge's "Duck Mother."

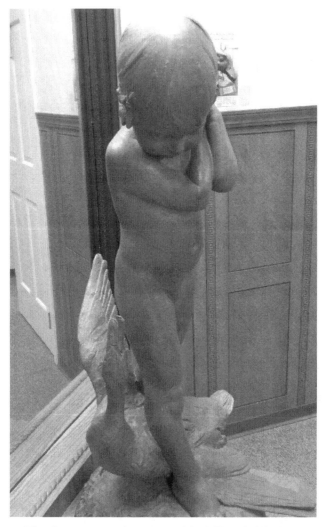

The bronze sculpture entitled "Duck Mother" was removed from the park and now resides in the village hall, in front of a large mirror from the old Fenton Hotel.
(Image from MVH)

The park suffered abuse and in 1950 the bronze statue was removed and hidden away in the Public Works Garage. About thirty years later, the head of the Department of Public Works found it, gave it an overall cleaning, and now it graces the hallway as one enters the Village Board Room. Because of a complaint about the small, nude statue where "everyone could see it," for several years it was draped with a beige crocheted shawl!

The fountain pond now blossoms with flowering bulbs in the spring and beautiful impatiens during the summer.

***

On Memorial Day, Sunday, May 30, 1948, members of Clute-Phillips Post #938, American Legion, honored those who have made the supreme sacrifice while serving their country with the dedication of their Veteran's Memorial in the southwest corner of the park. Rep. James W. Wadsworth of Geneseo, representing the 41st New York Congressional District was the principal speaker; Lester E. Searles of Lockport was soloist. Rev. Lieut. Emil C. Bongumil, Niagara County American Legion Chaplain, was in charge of the Legion ritual; Rev. Leonard P. Ives, Post Chaplain and pastor of the Middleport Methodist Episcopal Church was Master of Ceremonies. Roger M. Kinzly and William J. Holahan were dedication chairmen. The 3:00 pm ceremony was attended by about 500 people.

Granite boulder Veteran's Memorial in the Common on Park Ave.
(Image from MVH)

The memorial, a large granite boulder sitting atop a concrete base, has bronze plaques bearing the names of members of the community who gave their lives during the World Wars: "WWI: Grover Clute, Leo Fuery, Francis Manning, Thomas Phillips. WWII: Hugh Barlow, Wallace Campbell, Charles Daley, Francis Hickey, Donald Johnson, Fletcher Johnson, Wilfred Money, Glenn Mudge, Charles Peters, John Silsby, Gerald Swift. Erected by Clute-Phillips Post #938, American Legion, V-J Day 1947." A smaller adjoining plaque dedicated in 1985 lists the names of John O'Brien, Robert LaShier and Edwin Guild.

The boulder came from Hosmer Road, Town of Hartland, and was set with the assistance of the Hartland Highway Department, Ray Shaw in charge.

The first annual Memorial Day service in 1949 was a simple ceremony consisting of a service by the Post Chaplain, three volleys by the firing squad and the playing of Taps; the members marched from the village parking lot assembly point to the monument. The following year they were accompanied by the Firemen's Drum Corps. Each year since then on the designated Memorial Day, a ceremony is held at the monument before proceeding across the street to the program at the Firemen's Memorial.

The taller American flag pole is "in honor of all deceased members of Clute-Phillips Post #938, dedicated in 1982." The shorter flag pole "in memory of POW-MIA from all wars and conflicts, dedicated 2000," flies their flag.

American Legion sign honoring those serving from the
Royalton Hartland Central School District
(Image from MVH)

Also in the American Legion area, the blue painted sign reads "Village of Middleport residents honor the men and women in our armed forces from the Royalton-Hartland Central School District. Dedicated by the village Board of Trustees, July 4, 1991" during Operation Desert Storm.

On Memorial Day 1952 the Middleport Fire Department dedicated their memorial in honor of the deceased members of the department, and as a symbol of the protection that the community enjoys against constant danger of fire. The old fire alarm bell that was purchased in 1912 is suspended from an arch connecting two brick columns; an electric clock is mounted at the top of the arch.

The bell used to hang in a tower at the rear of the village hall and also rang the 9:00pm "curfew" for the village children. The tower was taken down in 1946 to make the parking lot at the rear of the stores on the west side of Main Street.

Former Mayor Frank E. Braddock, the only living member of the Village Board of Trustees at the time the bell was purchased, tolled the bell and recalled the early days when fire alarms were spread by means of a local church bell.

Gordon Lee, Albion, Past President of the Western New York Volunteer Firemen's Association, made the dedication; Earl S. Dodge, Newfane, Trustee of the NYSVFA, spoke briefly. Francis Whittaker, president of the Fire Department, placed the wreath; Francis Schilling, past Fire Chief, was Master of Ceremonies. Francis Kubatek was chairman of the building committee.

The names of the Board members engraved on the bell are John O'Shaughnessy, President; Frank Braddock, George Jackson, Stephen Sherman and Charles Snell.

Greetings from
Middleport, New York

Middleport Fire Department memorial with the old bell
from the fire tower.
(Image from MVH)

The Centennial

The weeklong Centennial Celebration provided a summer of excitement that has long been remembered. Middleport was incorporated in March 28, 1859, but the event was held August 29-September 3, 1959, in hopes of having good weather - and it did cooperate!! A representative of the John B. Rogers Producing Co. of Fostoria, OH came early in the summer to set up the schedules, and then returned in early August to be resident director.

MIDDLEPORT, NEW YORK

*Centennial logo for Middleport's celebration
in 1959.
(Image from MVH)*

89

A Centennial Headquarters was set up at 19 Main Street for business and the sale of stock certificates, historical booklets, derby and top hats, centennial ties, vests, and plates. Peddler permits and Centennial Belle buttons were available. For those who didn't want to participate in the beard growing contest (and there were some pretty fancy beards) shaving permits cost $1.00. Store windows displayed antique items.

A contest for the centennial seal, won by high school junior Donald Owen over eight other entrants, contrasted a mule-drawn canal barge of 1859 with a modern vessel, and appeared on the centennial china plates and stationery. The contest to name the four-evening pageant the "Towpath Story," submitted by freshman Sharon Walker, was selected from 137 entries. Letters were received from all over the county to be postmarked with the special die hub: "1859 Middleport 1959 Centennial Pageant Aug. 29 - Sept. 3".

On Fridays "wooden nickels" were legal tender at the stores, and the women wore their old-style apparel when on the street. A group of the Centennial Belles appeared on the Helen Neville TV program; several couples in "costume" visited neighboring village "restaurants" to advertise.

The festivities began with a Centennial Balloon the Royalton-Hartland Central School tennis courts on Saturday, August 29th, 9:00pm-1:00am with music by Tommy Rizzo's orchestra; old fashioned costumes were encouraged. Sunday was "church day"; a box lunch picnic supper on the school grounds, followed by a program of band music under

the direction of Robert Cavers, and choral renditions by
Mrs. Miriam Flatt's 100-voice choir.

*Citizens dressed in old-style apparel as they celebrate the
village's Centennial.
(Image from MVH)*

At the "American Heritage Day" program, colors
were posted by the American Legion color guard, remarks
by centennial co-chairmen William J. Holahan and Donald
Owen, and by Mayor Elton Birch, and an address by Lt. Col.
James R. Woods, Commanding Officer of the 1st Missile
Battalion, 4th Artillery Regt., Fort Niagara. A stirring
patriotic address was given by the Hon. William E. Miller of
Lockport, 40th Congressional District, who was a candidate
for Vice-President of the United States with Presidential
Candidate Barry Goldwater just five years later.

Parade float turning the corner onto Main Street with a jail, holding citizens who did not grow a beard for the centennial celebration.
(Image from MVH)

There was a huge Centennial Parade! Daytime activities during the week included an antique show, an art show, an old fashioned tea, a style show with seventy-five participants; the bake sale by the Centennial Belles had a professional auctioneer; an antique auto show, and a children's parade. In honor of "Pioneer Day" a long list of elder Middleport folk were recognized as being direct descendants of our early settlers.

There were twenty-three finalists in the Miss Middleport contest, based on pageant ticket sales. The winner was Mary Nicolia who reigned as queen of the celebration, attended by runners-up Barbara Cassett and Janet Whitney. The Queen was crowned by State Senator

Earl W. Brydges, and won a trip for her and a chaperone to the New Hampshire resort, Wentworth-by-the Sea.

Miss Middleport, Mary Nicolia riding in the middle, with Janet Whitney on her right and Barbara Cassett to her left.
(Image from MVH)

The pageant, "The Towpath Story" with five narrators - the Rev. Alfred L. Underhill, Mrs. Muriel Brewer, Mrs. Rose Gaughn, Charles Grinnell and Kenneth Schlinger, traced the growth of Middleport from the Frontier and Indian days through five major wars and many social eras, to the (then) present, with background musical selections. In the Civil War segment, the part of General Ely S. Parker, Secretary to General Ulysses S. Grant, was played by Chief Everett Parker of the Tonawanda Indian Reservation, the closest living descendant of General Parker.

Different organizations and groups in the village were assigned one of the seventeen scenes in the two-hour pageant. It was performed with a cast of 300, on a stage 250 feet long and 75 feet deep. Among the props were horses, wagons, teepees, canoes, campfires and antique cars. At the close of each of the four performances, lovely fireworks were under the direction of a representative from the American Fireworks Co. of Hudson, OH. Attendance averaged over 1000 per night, and after the third performance, it was reported that "our debts are all paid and we are operating in the black." <u>Good weather, hard work, and cooperation!!</u>

Streets

On the earliest map of Middleport, at the time of inception in 1859, the area north of the canal is the same as today except that a road extended from Mechanic Street along the canal, at least to the east village line.

Mill Street - named because of the location of the grist mill. Hartland Street - because it ran from the canal into the Town of Hartland.

Main Street ran north to Vernon Street; at that time Vernon St. ran straight north, and was the main street going out of town.

Main Street looking north towards the bridge circa 1908.
(Image from RHCL)

Terry Street - probably named for Abiel Terry, an early settler.

Sleeper Street - named for James and Solomon Sleeper who lived there.

Town Line Road ran west from Hartland Street, and the part of the village that lies north of this center line lies in the Town of Hartland. Now the name is Sherman Road, named for early resident Orange W. Sherman.

State Street was on the map, as was part of Liberty Street. The village exercised the right of eminent domain and forced the extension of Liberty Street from Maple Avenue to Vernon Street; it was extended to Main Street when the trolley went through.

State Street looking west towards Main Street from Vernon St.
(Image from RHCL)

The "Common Hall" - between Vernon and Main, now is the park.

Church Street - extended only as far as the creek. The street that is now South Hartland was shown.

Wall Street was between the cemetery and Vernon Street, by 1899 changed to Cemetery Street, and recently a continuation of Maple Avenue.

Vernon Street - extended over the railroad to what was later named South Street.

Vernon Street looking south from the railroad tracks.
(Image from RHCL)

Rail Road Street - extended from the railroad to just a short way north of Liberty Street.

The fifty-two acre Robertson Tract developed the whole area from Vernon Street east to the village limits, between State Street and the canal. Taken over by Hiram A. Robertson in 1860, he extended Rail Road Street to State Street and put in many trees; in 1897 the village was petitioned to rename the street Maple Avenue. He also put in the side streets - Robertson, Washington, William and East Avenue. East Canal Street followed the south side of the canal between Robertson and East Avenue.

The first street Commissioner was appointed in 1862 and was paid $425. This money was raised by taxes for repair and construction of streets. In 1887, it was suggested that the "name of each street be on a plain little sign at every three or four corners."

On the 1890 map, the present Route 31 was called Freeman Road, west of Main Street, no doubt because of the two Freeman families who lived at the end of Main Street.

Watson Avenue - extended from Kelly Avenue west to the village limits.

Church Street - extended from Main, west to Watson Avenue,

Van Etten Street - ran between Watson Avenue and the canal.

Centennial - ran from Watson Avenue, north to the canal.

Charles Street - named for C. Dunkin (the jeweler), went through his property, possibly now Carolyn Street.

What is now Kelly Avenue ran from Watson to the canal. Later it was continued south to the railroad, through the property of F. Kelly, and named Kelly Avenue.

Miller Avenue - continued on from the railroad south to Freeman Road, through the property of Nathaniel W. Miller. In 1929 it was renamed Kelly Avenue to conform to Kelly Avenue north of the tracks.

Orchard Street - was "from Church Street south to Freeman."

Francis Street - was from Main, west on the map,

Part of Alfred Street was on the map.

Elizabeth Street extended west from Rail Road Street, between Liberty and the railroad.

Main Street from the canal to Church Street, and State from Main to Vernon were paved with brick in 1915, and the speed limit that was set at eight miles per hour in 1908 was increased to fifteen miles per hour. The speed limit was raised to twenty miles per hour in 1922. In 1928 State Street from Alfred to Vernon was widened and was paved with brick because it didn't have to season before use, as concrete paving did. Many of the side street were paved in the 1920s and bonds were approved to cover the cost. Grading and concreting of the Main Street hill was done.

Stop signs were being considered where there was heavy traffic.

The speed limit was raised to thirty miles per hour in 1941; parking spaces were marked with white lines; no parking was allowed within 10 feet of hydrants; cars could not be parked on the sidewalks or left parked on the street all night. In the early 1950s, new stop signs were put at the intersection of Park Avenue and Main Street, and at State Street and the Vernon Street bridge.

For ten years our streets were in a constant state of "rebuilding." Approved in 1994, Routes 31E and 271 were rebuilt from the Jeddo Creek Bridge to the Orleans County line, and the sidewalk engineers were all agog because the head of the bridge project was "a girl!"

State project rebuilding Route 31E (State Street).
(Image from MVH)

The work that began in April 1995 not only rebuilt and paved the streets, but included relocation of water lines and street lighting, adjustment of manholes, the installation of new sidewalks and storm sewer drainage, and in some areas new sanitary sewer lines, and removal of dead trees. The replacement trees were placed on the inner side of the walks, becoming the responsibility of the property owner, who could select the type of tree from several choices.

The village was allowed to select antique-style lighting and brick inlaid sidewalks, enhancing the village's "old canal town" image. The basic work was completed by September even though at a few intersections telephone poles were in the street. This two-year project was part of a $3 million New York State Department of Transportation program to standardize the state highway system.

In 1996 the village Department of Public Works replaced the waterline and storm sewer, sidewalks and curbing in an area of Church Street.

In the summer of 1998 another New York State Department of Transportation project redid Route 31 from the Day Road at Lockport to the Orleans County line. The $12.5 million project was a scheduled two-year program with Keeler Construction Company, Albion, the contractor. Later, new sidewalks were put in on the north side, and on the south side of Telegraph Road from the theater to the drug store as the road shoulder was cut from eight to four feet.

In 2003 the Village Department of Public Works rebuilt Park Avenue from Alfred Street to Maple Avenue, correcting the drainage and placing new curbing, and removing the trolley tracks that were covered 60 years ago, supposedly a temporary measure.

In the early days, in case of fire, one hoped that a neighbor would have a full cistern of water. Reservoirs were built under the streets to help distribute water around the village; the first one was built at the southwest corner of Vernon Street and Park Avenue in 1888. The reservoir was filled at the time the school on Park Avenue burned, but it was in bitterly cold weather and the water was frozen.

The reservoir on the north side of Francis Street near Kelly Avenue was built in 1895; the one on the east side of S. Main Street at #97 was built in 1897. One was also built on the west side of S. Vernon Street between lots #41 and #42. The Reservoir on the south side of Park Avenue between lots #39 and #41 apparently had a spring beneath it as in 1909 there was difficulty in keeping the cement floor intact.

Roads

Our Stone Road was originally a plank road and a toll road. They were connectors between farm communities and a nearby canal town. Between 1844 and 1855, 350 plank roads were built totaling nearly 3000 miles.

In 1856 five directors were selected for the Middleport and Ridge Road Plank Road Co. The roads were made of 3-inch planks, 8-feet long, laid end-to-end across the road, with the center a few inches higher to permit water runoff. The cost would be about $2000 per mile; toll roads were incorporated for their building and maintenance.

After a few years these roads needed constant repair, and were gradually covered over with gravel. During the two-year term of John Kinyon, Jr., as Highway Commissioner (of the Town of Hartland), this became a crushed "stone" road.

The McAdam process of road building was conceived in about 1906, and the experimental road using this method was the seven-mile stretch of Griswold Street, from Route 31 to Wolcottville.

A stone crusher was set up at the quarry near Mountain Road and special heavy machinery was purchased, including four road engines with about three times the horsepower of threshing engines, and three heavy-duty wide-wheeled cars that could each carry twenty-one yards of crushed stone, as opposed to the team and wagon that could carry only one yard at a time. Dust from the road got into the driving gears of the engines requiring frequent greasing, and a twenty-five pound can of cup grease was used every day.

Unable to make more than eleven round-trips a day, the crews stayed alternate nights in Middleport and Wolcottsville. According to Paul Murphy who worked on the project, it required a couple of years to finish the road and then it had to harden and cure before being used.

Road graders were often landowners who did road work for credit towards their taxes. Among this crew are members of the author's family, starting from the left her Grandfather Ora Brewer, Father Raymond Brewer and Uncle Earl Brewer working on Johnny Cake Road now known as Lincoln Avenue Extension.
(Image from RTH)

Housing

When the time came that there were few village building lots available, small developments provided more room for housing.

In the early 1950s a street was cut through a vacant piece of land west of East Avenue; it was named Butler Parkway as Mr. & Mrs. Bert Butler were the first to build on the street. In the mid-1950s with real estate agent Paul J. Hammond as the moving force, Hammond Parkway was developed with room for 12 building lots, across from the (then) elementary school.

Chase Brown of Lockport started the Old Mill Trailer Park on Sherman Road beginning with 20 homes, in 1958.

Locust Drive, the street lined with locust trees, was developed in the 1960s by Levi Yoder & Sons, with room for 12 lots on the eight acre plot between the Lutheran Church and the Drive-In Theater.

Edgewood Manor Estates off Kelly Avenue was developed by James Coppola of Edgewood Manor Corp. and Herbert Schneider of S & C Development Corp. The tract provided 26 building lots, the houses built by Duracraft Homes. Manor Lane became a dedicated street in 1967.

A four-apartment house was erected on Pebble Court, just off Stone Road at Sleeper Street in the 1970s, by builder Lawrence Krolak. Later another was built at the end of the street. Maedl Lane was opened when builder Robert Maedl built an apartment house just off Sleeper Street.

A ribbon cutting for the Middleport Country Estates complex located on three acres of land at 89 Telegraph Road opposite Kelly Avenue was held on September 7, 1986. It consists of 24 one-bedroom and one two-bedroom units of senior citizen subsidized housing, a portion of which are designed for the handicapped. A multi-purpose center with kitchen facilities serves as a gathering place for the residents.

The units are available to persons of age sixty-two or older and/or handicapped who meet the income requirements. The developer was ITC Corporation of Niagara Falls, a non-profit group.

Construction for a like complex, Middleport Villa Estates, developed by Dr. Irene Elia of Middleport Limited Partnership began in July 1987.

Middleport Villa Estates on Telegraph Road begins construction. The complex was planned with twenty-five units designed for seniors or handicapped residents. (Image from Lockport Union Sun and Journal)

Village Water

The idea that developed into the Middleport Water Company in 1911 came when Theodore Dosch, the first manager of the Niagara Sprayer Company and attorney George Sheldon found the springs on the high ground near the village. They engineered a system of piping water underground to hydrants.

A bond issue of $48,000 was approved for installation of the village water system, and $57,000 for construction of the village sewer system; both contracts were let to Cusano & Dower. A celebration was held at the Fenton Hotel on January 30, 1913 to commemorate the satisfactory testing of the hydrants.

A bond issue in 1919 was approved for construction of a dam, reservoir and filtration plant. There were three main sources of water: the springs at the west plant on the Mountain Road, the filtration plant directly south of the village on the Freeman Road, and in an emergency, the Erie Barge Canal. In late summer when the ground water sources were low, canal water supplemented the water at the reservoir and residents were notified to boil their water.

In 1949, water was pumped into the new 25,000,000 gallon reservoir through the emergency water line that had just been completed instead of being pumped directly into the village mains, and for the first time, boiling was no longer necessary. Now it was chlorinated at the Centennial Street Station when pumped from the canal, then passed through the filtration plant where it was chlorinated again. The west plant operated at night, and the Freeman Road plant during the day. The spring water was chlorinated at the pumping station that also controlled the supply in the 70,000 gallon standpipe on Griswold Street.

Checks of the water were made every few hours by a representative of the State Public Health System, and samples were inspected by the State Board of Health at Albany.

The Niagara County Water District was formed in 1958, and by 1999 we were purchasing water from them in addition to our primary sources, at the time, the well on Mountain Road. Our tap water met all New York State drinking water health standards.

For the fourth straight year, Middleport came in first in the Niagara County Blind Taste Test Challenge held at the Lockport Mall on May 13, 1994. The village also participated in the New York State testing for lead and copper, and came through with flying colors.

In 2001, the village closed the ground water well by a directive of the State, although with chlorination there was no problem with the quality of the water. In 2002, just over 70 million gallons were purchased and used through 676 connections serving 1917 people.

During 2002 and 2003 the water meters were changed to new radio read meters which took only about an hour to read rather than two days.

Sewage Treatment Plant

The seed-idea for a new village sewage treatment plant facility was planted in 1963 when New York State reported pollution in the west branch of Jeddo Creek. The construction of one of the first secondary treatment plants conforming to New York State standards in the four-county area of Niagara, Orleans, Erie, and Genesee began in July 1968 and was ready for use in January 1970.

The new plant cost $1,050,000; about 30% was state funded under the Pure Waters Program, and another 30% through the Federal Environmental Protection Agency. Located on N. Hartland Street it has a capacity of 700,000 gallons per day, using the trickling filter method fed through a new eighteen-inch sewer main. The old plant was built in 1912, rated at 75,000 gallons per day are handled an average 300,000 gallon daily - inadequate in both capacity and technique.

Laur & Mack Contracting Co., Inc. of Niagara Falls was the general contractor, and Wendel Associates of Lockport were consulting engineers and planners. Guest speaker at the official opening ceremony on September 18, 1971, was Assemblyman V. Sumner Carroll of Niagara Falls.

Groundbreaking ceremonies for the new sewage plant were held in 1968 with officials, engineers and village mayor Elton Birch, third from the left.
(Image from MVH)

Progress on the building of the sewage plant less than a month after groundbreaking.
(Image from MVH)

Refuse

In 1951 the same as now, "savings have to be made somewhere," and village employees took over the collection of ashes and refuse which had been done satisfactorily by local Voelker Brothers: refuse on Tuesday, ashes on Thursday during the coal burning season; rubbish on the first Thursday of each month. A contract at the same rate of $20 per pickup on Monday nights at 7:00pm, was renewed with Elmer "Baldy" Burr, who fed the garbage to his pigs. Since 1930 the village had owned two acres on the Dublin Road in the Town of Shelby which was used as the dump. The old village dump was on the west side of Griswold Street, on the north side of the hill, probably where the stone quarry was when the road was macadamized in 1908.

In 1968 a contract for weekly garbage collection was made with Harry Goodrich of Lyndonville. Monthly trash pickup was made by the village. The village dump on the Dublin Road was closed by Orleans County and New York State in 1970, and a contract was made with Goodrich & Son for garbage and trash collection. Collections were made on Thursday mornings, this eventually led to a 5:00pm Wednesday dog quarantine as the dogs molested the garbage bags set out the evening before.

J&I Disposal of Akron had the contract for several years; BPI Niagara Sanitation for several years, with curbside recycling beginning in 1996. "NEI" - National Environmental Inc., received the Contract in 2003.

Telephone

The Atlantic & Pacific Telegraph office was located in the J. Compton store in 1871; W. A. Austin was the operator. In the fall of 1890 the Postal Telegraph Co. was setting up poles for a new line. We are not sure when the Bell Telephone Co. came here, but it was about 1900. The cable stretched from the west side of Main Street to the pole on Vernon St., a distance of 255 feet. This cost $1789 with the old style wooden-mounted wall phone. To use it, one turned the crank to connect to the operator, who asked "number please?" and then made the connection from the switchboard. In 1901, the cranks were removed from the telephones at Buffalo due to a new invention which permitted calling the operator by just lifting the receiver.

The Town of Hartland had no telegraph or telephone, and Bell had refused to provide a line except at exorbitant rates. A young newspaper man, Mr. E. B. Crosby from Lockport, purchased a grove of chestnut trees and in less than a week, five men had the poles ready for the eight miles of line from Jeddo to Middleport via Johnson's Creek. A gang of twelve farmers planted them while experts strung the wire in a few days.

One morning the Bell agent was surprised to see the poles approaching the village, and by that evening ten stations were on the line, paying the nominal sum of $25 per year. At a meeting with Bell, Mr. Crosby was threatened with having another line alongside his.

In 1901, poles were set for the Home Telephone Co. and by August the 150 subscribers gave Middleport three telephone companies, including Bell and Hartland Telephone. Apparently the Hartland line didn't survive for long as we've never seen reference to it again. By fall the Independent Home Co. was offering its patrons all night service with connections to the fire alarm. By notifying the operator, the location of the fire could be sent in immediately.

Businesses had to have both the Bell and Home phones, each with a different number, as the two companies were not inter-connected. By the end of the year, the local branch of the Home Telephone Co. was purchased by the Continental Long Distance Telegraph Co.

The area dial telephones were installed in 1938 at Middleport and Gasport, apparently a trial run on a small customer base. Lockport, with 10,000 customers, received their dial system in 1951.

The first rate increase in twenty years was granted to the New York Telephone Co. in 1950. The residential private lines cost $3.25, four-party lines and rural lines, $2.50. Business private lines were $5.50, two-party lines, $4.75, and rural lines, $3.75. Middleport subscribers could now call 1550 phones without a toll.

The Middleport numbers received five digits, all beginning with six, and this was the first step in the program to allow for direct dialing over a wider area. In 1963, Direct Distance Dialing connected eighty-three million telephones across the country. The central office building on Vernon St. was enlarged to handle a 70% increase in volume as the daily volume had doubled in five years. Five-cent tolls were cancelled on Middleport-Medina calls. When the numbers were changed to a "two letter-five numeral" plan, the Middleport office was assigned Republic-5, now "735."

In December 1980, the new all-electronic switching system was activated here: touch-tone phones with push buttons instead of dials offered greater speed in placing calls. A group of "custom calling" features became available: three-way calling, call forwarding, speed calling and call waiting. Middleport became the 32nd electronic central office in Western New York. Eventually all 14,000 central offices in the nationwide Bell System would be totally electronic.

Those strange looking Radio Relay Antenna Towers, like the one on Mountain Road, are spaced about thirty miles apart to speed travel of the long distance calls and television programs.

Electricity

The Middleport Power Co. was organized in 1899 under the leadership of William J. Sterritt, a prominent Middleport businessman, and Frank H. Dudley of Niagara Falls. The company utilized the old heading mill and dam at the outlet to the second pond on Middleport Creek, and at considerable expense and with little success, started the first electric power built in Middleport. The plant was operated by a water wheel and a steam engine.

The Middleport Gas & Electric Co. was formed in 1901 by Dudley & Johnson, who purchased the plant and contracted with the village for street lights. Up until this time the streets only had kerosene lamps on posts at each corner. A lamplighter kept the lamps filled with oil, trimmed the wicks, cleaned the chimneys, lighted the lamps at night and turned them out with morning light.

In 1906, twenty Middleport men invested $500 each to buy the Middleport Gas & Electric Co., and they supplied the village with electricity. Later service was extended to Gasport, Hartland Corners and Royalton Center, serving the country through which the lines passed. On April 12, 1910, the switches on the new transformer station were turned on and the streets were illuminated with the Westinghouse system of street lighting. On April 21, 1911, a dinner was tendered the Middleport businessmen by the Middleport Gas and Electric Company in commemoration of bringing Niagara Falls power to the village. In 1918, the men purchased the Newfane Electric Co., and lines were built to Newfane, Olcott and Appleton.

The names of the twenty men were: George F. Thompson, George R. Sheldon, Jeremiah Tracey, Stephen Sherman, John H. Gould, Everett A. Pearce, Edgar Knapp, Truman Jennings, Alfred Cooper, Thomas R. Hammond, John J. Jackson, Dennis L. Priesch, Patrick J. Fermoile, Frank M. Smith, John J. Mack, John O'Shaughnessy, Frank Braddock, John Benson, Elgie J. Lewis and Frank Tracey.

In 1922 the Lockport & Newfane Power and Water Supply Co. was also purchased, and the stockholders voted to consolidate the three companies under the name of Lockport & Newfane Power & Water Supply Company, which became part of the Ontario District, Buffalo Niagara Corporation. Long-range plans for modernization of its distribution system through Western New York started in 1929 at a cost of many millions of dollars.

Seventy percent of the changeover from 25-cycle to 60-cycle service was completed when work had to be suspended because of WWII. A three-year program was started as soon after the war as materials were available, and was scheduled to be completed by the end of 1950. Middleport was the first community selected for the changeover because it is located close to the path of the new high-voltage 60-cycle line which was built as a pre-requisite to the start of the program. Changing from 25 to 60-cycle eliminated flickering lights and made for more efficient operation of motors.

Before the actual changeover could be done, new substations had to be built at strategic points. A reconstructed circuit formed a big loop encircling eastern Niagara County and part of western Orleans County. The loop could carry 34,500 volts as opposed to the old 12,000 volts used on the 25-cycle system, and power could be provided from several points in the event of storms.

The loop is connected to the big 115,000 volt line that runs from Niagara Falls to Syracuse at a new transmission station built at Alabama Junction. From there it passes to the Telegraph Road station at Middleport, where the voltage is reduced to 34,500 volts for distribution to the loop. At the substation on Salt Works Road the voltage is reduced to 4800 volts for distribution to large industrial customers, as does the one at South and South Vernon Streets, Middleport.

When the entire changeover was completed, power was available from the Brockport end of the 34,500 volt loop, or from the southern end of the loop at Alabama Junction. This is designed to eliminate low-voltage problems at distant points from the "main line."

During the summer of 1948, the task of altering electric appliances in Middleport was undertaken; by spring 1949 the project was finished.

In 1950 the Buffalo Niagara Electric Corp., the Central New York Power Corp. and the New York Power & Light Corp. were reorganized into the Niagara Mohawk Power Corporation. After fifty-five years as Niagara Mohawk Power Corp., they and four other companies were bought by a British company in 2002, and in October 2005 under a single common global identification, they became known as National Grid.

Middleport Fire Department

The Compton Opera House burned in 1876, and the east side of Main Street burned in 1878 and again in 1879. The Lockport newspaper stated that "what Middleport needs most is an efficient fire department. The Firemen's Fund Insurance Co. has cancelled all their business risks in the Village on the grounds that the citizens have not taken adequate measures for their own protection from fire."

In 1884 the Wm. J. Sterritt Engine Co. with twenty-three members, the L. H. Spalding Hose Co. with seventeen men, and the A. D. Rich Hook & Ladder Co. with twenty men were merged, forming the beginning of the Middleport Fire Department. The village authorized $550 for a hose cart, buckets, etc; soon afterwards, fire struck the rented building and all materials were destroyed. The first Middleport Firemen's Day was established in 1884; this included a grand street parade, a baseball game and yacht races, and closed with a grand ball at the Opera House. Traditional field days were an annual rite for ninety-one years! There were many years when 10,000-15,000 people packed the main streets of the village.

The Firemen's Building was erected in 1891. A $6500, 1893 horse drawn steam fire engine made by the American Fire Engine Co. of Seneca Falls, NY, was purchased in 1895 for $3000, as it had been a floor model at the Chicago Exposition, representing the latest fire fighting technology. It has been said that $5 was offered to the first team of horses to respond at a fire. After having had the experience, the draft horses standing at the New York Central Railroad station were said to start off in the direction of the fire house at the sound of the alarm.

Affectionately called "the Steamer" it was retired from service in 1920, and for a half-century it faced an uncertain fate. In 1980 two members of the department undertook the project of restoring it, and it now stands in the recreation hall "as an icon of the department's proud history and tradition, and its deep seated roots in the community." It is one of the few remaining "steamers" in our region.

Sterritt Steamer being shown during parade in Middleport.
(Image from MVH)

A 300 pound fire bell was installed in a bell tower, and in 1898 the new bell and tower were engulfed in flames. After electricity was installed in 1902, a striking arm was placed in the bell tower of the Episcopal Church, and it became the fire alarm. The village paid $25 a year for its use.

In 1922 the L. H. Spalding Hose Co., the A. D. Rich Hook Co., and the W. J. Sterritt Engine Co. passed resolutions to disband and to unite as one company - the Middleport Fire Company. Soon the mechanized equipment was purchased. The early parade uniforms included straw hats, white shirts and white pants, and black shoes and bow ties.

L.H. Spalding Hose Co. was one of the three companies that would eventually become the Middleport Fire Company.
(Image from MVH)

In 1949, the Fire Department voted to sponsor the Cub Scouts, they still do today. Nearly sixty years of sponsorship is an enviable record! The Ladies Auxiliary donated twelve home monitors for the men in 1970, adding Middleport to the other companies in Niagara County with this latest communications system. Today, almost all of the active men have monitors in their homes.

To better serve more frequent first aid and rescue calls, the first vehicle for that purpose was purchased in 1974. First aid training began in 1938. Both the firemen and auxiliary served countless volunteer hours during the "Blizzard of '77," helping people in many ways. All available snowmobiles were put into use. Routinely, they are all are on hand with windstorms and trees down, electric power outages and flooding, etc.

From the beginning the Fire Department has always tried to improve by updating with better and more modern equipment and with continuous training of their men. They now have a fleet of state-of-the-art fire and rescue equipment worth over a million dollars. They provide emergency services, including interior structural fire fighting, technical rescue and advanced emergency medical care. They work closely with Tri-Town Volunteer Ambulance Service on local calls.

Tri-Town Ambulance

Before the days when "real" ambulance service was available in rural areas, emergency transport was handled by the funeral homes, as their vehicles were adaptable and their personnel were always available. The hearse doubled as an ambulance by removing the window curtains and adding a siren and a flashing light.

Richardson and Kneubel handled emergencies as early as 1930, and Wallace & Heath continued the service from 1946 until the mid-1960s, when they gave the village a one-year notice that their ambulance insurance would be cancelled on the next December 31st. At the deadline, the village contracted with the Village of Medina to fill the immediate gap in service.

In 1967, two firemen saw the need for the ambulance service and a group of citizens from Hartland and Gasport spent many months in meetings investigating the requirements for furnishing volunteer ambulance service, and an application for the charter was made to the state.

A charter was received to operate in October 1968, but an ambulance had to be purchased and crew members assembled and trained in the use of the equipment and in basic first aid. In the very beginning, the ambulance was stationed at crew members' homes or at the Hartland Town Garage or at the Gasport Fire Hall. As more members were added from the Middleport area, a rotating schedule was set up including the Middleport Fire Hall. Calls were received at a Gasport nursing home, and then relayed to crew members at their homes. In 1972 a base station was installed at the Niagara County Sheriff's office, and calls were relayed to the crew members via home monitors.

First ambulance for the Tri Town Ambulance service back in 1968. The crew from left to right are Merlin Frasier, Norm Frasier, Flossie Arnold and Barb Walker. (Image from files of the ambulance company by Joe Ognibene)

In 1970 construction began at 8935 Ridge Road on a garage/meeting building, most of the work done by the crew members. The Village of Middleport donated land and a second building was erected on S. Hartland St. in 1975; a third building on State St., Gasport, was built in 1979.

Crew members are given extensive training, and some of them are qualified Red Cross instructors, and some are EMT instructors. Service is available to the areas covered by the Hartland, Gasport, Middleport and Terry's Corners fire districts, an area of 92.8 square miles. Subscriptions of $40 per year provide the operating base for the service.

EMT candidates have to be 18 years of age, and attend a six-month class at Niagara County Community College or Niagara University. Drivers have to be at least twenty-one years old.

Middleport Saving And Loan

The Middleport Savings and Loan was organized in October, 1922, and temporary officers were elected to serve until the first annual election. Assets were about $5000. The first regular meeting place association was the office of the Middleport Gas and Electric Co. on State Street where collection of funds from members were received Monday evenings between 5:30-8:30pm. Business was conducted there for five years.

In 1932, the former offices of the Community Trust Company, housed in the Fenton Hotel, became the new home of the Middleport Savings and Loan. After several more changes they would move into a new brick building on the canal and eventually merged with Anchor Bank. (Image from RTH)

In 1927, the Middleport Savings and Loan Association moved to the office in the village building on Main Street, now the police office. In 1932, the office moved to the building formerly occupied by the Community Trust Company in the end of the Fenton Hotel. In June 1945, they again leased the village building. During the "bank holidays" of 1931, 1932, and 1933 the doors of the Savings and Loan remained open.

Cramped for space, the office again moved in January 1963 to the newly opened office of the Jackling & Shaw Insurance Agency, 15 Main Street, in the former drug store building. At the annual meeting in 1974, two veteran directors retired because of age requirements: Clifford McDonald who had served as a director for the association's fifty-one years with the title of Chairman Emeritus, and Edward Phillips a thirty-seven-year director who had served as treasurer for fourteen years as Treasurer Emeritus.

On April 1, 1976, the Middleport Savings and Loan, with assets of $2.5 million, merged with the Niagara First Savings and Loan, Tonawanda, with James A. Soldwisch as president, and William C. Shaw, former president of the Middleport Savings and Loan as vice-president in charge of the Middleport office. In June, 1976, they moved into the new brick building erected for the Middleport office, across the corner of Main and State Street on the canal. The new staff included Mrs. Sandra L. Genet, assistant manager, and Mrs. Geraldine Barnum. In 1981 Mrs. Genet was named manager. Mr. Shaw retired in 1981, remaining vice-president and director.

Niagara First Savings and Loan merged with Anchor Savings Bank until 1982, with Mrs. Genet remaining as manager until being transferred to manage the Batavia office in 1986. In 1991, Anchor closed the Middleport office, merging all their business to their Albion office.

Commercial Banking

The Lockport Daily Journal reported on Sept. 19, 1871 that the Lockport Bank had recently opened at Blakslee & Hoyt (on Main Street, Middleport), but we have seen nothing further about it. We have seen "there was at one time a banking institution here, but the financial pressures of 1877 caused it to suspend operation."

In 1889, C. B. Taylor was noted as a private banker, corner of Main and State Streets, "the only banking institution in the place." This bank was operated in conjunction with a drug store and both were taken over by Harvey Hoag.

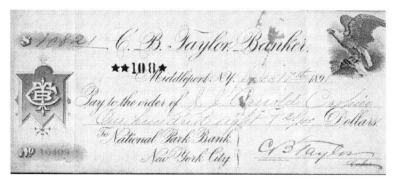

Private bank note from C.B. Taylor who operated out of his drug store.
(Image from MVH)

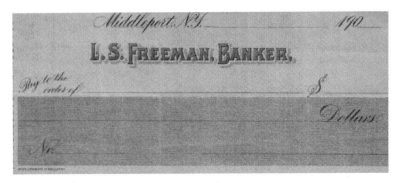

Private bank note from L.S.Freeman.
(Image from MVH)

Linus S. Freeman operated a private bank in Middleport from 1892 until his death in 1908. In 1894 he moved into the new Delano store at 12 Main Street. A wagon had been sent to Buffalo to bring down an 8000 pound vault; four horses were required to move it. A plate glass window had to be removed to get the vault in the building, and "the usual committee of 47 were on hand with suggestions."

In 1908 the First National Bank was formed and ready to open by August 1st. George R. Sheldon was president, Edgar Knapp was vice-president, John J. Mack was cashier. Additional directors were Theodore Dosch and Elgie J. Lewis and later, Roy L. Wheeler. The bank opened in the office of the late Linus S. Freeman.

About 1919 they built the present bank building at the corner of Main Street and Park Avenue. The bank remained in operation until December 17, 1931, when most of the small banks in this area closed. Within a year they had paid their second dividend to depositors totaling 54%.

The Community Trust Company was opened as another bank in Middleport in 1924. George D. Judson was President Charles R. Richardson, secretary, and Rockwell H. Comfort was cashier; there were twelve other directors. They were located in the west end of the Fenton Hotel. Warren M. Snell soon joined the bank and was made assistant cashier.

When the smaller size currency was brought out, it was on display in the State Street window for a month before being distributed to the public in July 10, 1929. The new bills were 2-11/16 inches compared to the old 3-3/16 inches.

The bank closed its doors in 1931 prior to the "bank holiday." In total, they repaid 80% to their depositors by the end of 1933. Plans were under way to liquidate the remaining assets, enabling payment of 100%.

In 1934 the Niagara County National Bank & Trust Company of Lockport, a Marine Midland bank, purchased the previously owned First National Bank building and opened a branch here on September 26th, with Warren M. Snell as manager.

Interior view of the Niagara County National Bank and Trust Company of Lockport offices on Main and Park. That building was erected in 1919 and Key Bank was the last occupant until 2015.
(Image from RTH)

In 1951, many of the banks in Western New York merged with the Marine Trust Company of Western New York who now operated fifty-one offices in nineteen western New York communities, the largest bank outside of New York City. The local bank became the Middleport Office of the Marine Trust Company of Western New York.

In 1980, Marine Midland became a member of the HSBC Group, a worldwide financial services company with headquarters in London. (HSBC stands for Hong Kong Shanghai Banking Corporation, and there were many jokes about receiving chopsticks for dividends). In 1994, Marine Midland adopted the red and white bow tie logo, replacing their stylized ship design. It wasn't until 1999 that the branch names were changed to HSBC. They now have 5500 offices in seventy-nine countries and territories.

The Middleport Federal Credit Union held its organizational meeting in 1975 at the Iron Horse Restaurant, with its first annual meeting in December at the Middleport Fire Hall. Officers were elected for 1976; there were 152 members. This was the first community chartered credit union in New York State. FMC was the first company to provide deductions for credit union members; the office was at the home of the treasurer. A credit union is similar to a bank except that its members own and operate it. There has been a dispute between the credit unions and the fee-charging industry, as they don't pay the taxes to which banks are subject.

In February 1978, the credit union moved their office to 20 Main Street in the Masonic building. To become a member, one had to live or work in the town of Royalton or Hartland. In 1988, their membership was at 890. In 1992, the 17-year-old Middleport Credit Union and the thirty-five year old Unit #1 Federal Credit Union of Lockport merged, and the Middleport office was moved into the former Anchor Savings Bank building on State Street. On May 15th a grand opening celebration, cookout and family jamboree was held at the Middleport branch.

Ranking high for safety, strength and performance the credit union earned five-star ratings. In 2003 Unit #1

Federal Credit Union changed its name to Cornerstone Community Federal Credit Union, and membership was open to anyone who lives, works, worships, and goes to school or volunteers in Niagara County.

Post Office

Records show that a post office was established at Middleport on March 25, 1825. James Northam was the first postmaster, and as his store was on the canal, undoubtedly the office was in his store. The second postmaster, 1829-1841, was Alden S. Baker, an employee of Mr. Northam who had purchased the store.

Prior to the establishment of postal routes in this area, the nearest post office was in Batavia. Philip Freeman, who lived at Freeman's Corners, had said that before there was a post office here, he walked to Ridgeway to pick up mail. That was the first post office in Orleans County, established on the Ridge Road in 1816.

We don't know the location of all our offices: in 1861 it was in the drug store of Dr. F. L. Taylor and everything was lost when four stores burned. Fernando Hinchey became postmaster in 1888, and the post office was in his store on the west side of Main Street. He died the following year, and his wife became postmistress and their son, John, became her deputy.

Interior view of the work area of the Middleport Post Office in 1921. Workers are identified from left to right as Julio Hammond, Tom Steen and Postmaster Tom Hammond who served from 1914 – 1922.
(Image from the Wm. Holahan collection and Miss Anne Hammond)

In 1897 the post office was in the W. D. Hoyt Candy Store at 31 Main Street. Two nights before Christmas, the safe was blown, and in the robbery $600 in postage and $100 cash was lost. The stamp inventory was higher than usual for mailings to the folks who were prospecting for gold in the Alaskan Klondike. A neighbor saw three men running down the street after the explosion, but in the dark identity was not possible. A team of horses and a sleigh had been stolen from a nearby farmer; the sleigh was found abandoned in Erie County.

A twenty foot addition was later made to the east end of the building, providing a separate area for the post office.

In 1921 the office was still in the same location. On the 1931 insurance map the post office was at 21 Main Street, and remained there until the present one was built.

One county in each state was chosen as a Rural Free Delivery experimental site, and in New York State, Genesee County was selected in 1896. When John A. Merritt III of Lockport was United States Post Master General in 1898; Rural Free Delivery was established in Niagara County. Three years later there were forty-two Rural Free Delivery routes in this area. The average length of the route was twenty-two miles, and carriers received $500 a year, and were allowed to deliver papers so long as it didn't interfere with the efficiency of the mail service.

In the fall of 1901 Eli Clark was assigned Route #35, extending from north of the village to Millers, County Line and north of Johnson's Creek. William B. Burghardt had Route #36, extending south to Reynolds' Tavern. George S. Helenbold had Route #37 extending south on Griswold Street and east to West Shelby.

Three routes started out from Gasport, and one from Wolcottsville. The post office at Johnson's Creek was discontinued and the mail was sent through Middleport. Harry Shaw was the carrier for Route #38 from Johnson's Creek to Middleport, including the area northwest of Middleport.

Postal wagons were used by rural carriers, and from pictures that we have, they looked like a large oblong box mounted on large wagon type wheels, or sled-type runners for winter. Middleport had four postal wagons.

Middleport Post Office at the corner of Church and Main St.
(Image from RTH)

Our brick Colonial Revival style post office at 42 Main Street, done under a Works Progress Administration) WPA Project, was opened in January 1941. The contractor was Smythe & Company of Tacoma Park, Maryland. The lot on which it is built was occupied by the trolley depot on the south, and behind it the Universalist Church sheds; on the north side of the lot was the home that had been the Methodist Church parsonage from 1845-1915.

The mural on the south wall, "Rural Highway," was done by Marianne Appel, a Buffalo art teacher, also under a WPA Project. It was refurbished in 1995. A bench for the foyer was given by the Gasport Lions Club. The handicapped access ramp was built in 2004.

The post office was placed on the National Historic Register in 1989.

Middleport was promoted from a third class to a second class office in 1922. In 1926, we were given regular city delivery; in 1950, once-daily delivery replaced the former twice-daily. Two drive-up boxes, local and out-of-town, were placed at the curb in 1973. Possibly not "government issue," but for many years red and green light bulbs were in the lampposts during the Christmas season, and a small drop box was put out for "Letters to Santa."

The post office was the center of activity in 1986 when Middleport hosted the First Day Issue for the 19¢ Belva Lockwood stamp with ceremonies at the high school.

Possibly not too many postmasters now recall the days when small orders of baby chicks were delivered by parcel post instead of Railway Express, although it still happens in rural areas. It was fun to go into our post office when the "cheep, cheeps" were coming from the boxes of yellow balls of fluff - probably as long as you weren't in the post office all day!

In 2000, the post office changed to automatic mail sorting that was done out of the Buffalo office. For mailing purposes Route 31 within the village limits remained Telegraph Road, as the recently adopted "Rochester Road" would not be recognized as the proper address.

Middleport Free Library

Historical records relate that as far back as 1823, the area was served by a floating library boat that traveled the Erie Canal, lending books under the sponsorship of E & E Wilcox Encyclopedia of Albany.

In 1831, subscriptions were taken for $3 each to establish a library at Middleport. It was not until 1873 when the first Middleport Library Association was formed under the direction of Rev. James E. Dennis, who had just come to the Episcopal Church. Books were donated by local citizens, and these books were housed in a room at the Pierce Hotel at least for a few years.

No mention of a library here was made again until 1928 when the formation of the Middleport Free Library was begun in earnest by a group of local people under the influence of the Middleport Study Club. In January 1929, a reading room was opened in a small upstairs room on the balcony of the Universalist Parish Hall. Again, with donated books the reading room spread into a library, and the Middleport Free Library opened on March 23, 1929. Mrs. Marjorie Reynolds, a member of the Study Club, was the prime mover.

There was no one in Middleport with library training, so Mrs. Reynolds contacted the New York State Library to determine the minimum requirements for a librarian of a small public library. By going to summer school and library workshops, the librarian could be educated as a professional. People were very generous with their time, and Edna Allgrunn served as a helper for several years. A charter was issued by the State of New York on July 19, 1929.

The Middleport Study Club, prime movers in establishing a library in the 1920s, is shown here in a 1952 newspaper clipping. They continued to be an active club until the 1970s.
(Image from Medina Journal Register)

When library status was received from the New York State Library, it moved to a room in the Niagara Herald building at the corner of Main and Mill Streets. In 1933, the Village offered the use of what later became the police office. In 1937 the Middleport Free Library was given the highest rating in its class by the State of New York. When space became crowded, the Library Board began looking for a permanent location.

Dedication of the Vernon Street library property on November 11, 1945.
(Image from MVH)

The present property at 9 S. Vernon Street was a gift from Mr. & Mrs. Robert Stilts; Mr. Stilts was the president of the Robertson Lumber Company. Library Board member emeritus Gladys Kinzly was the Stilts' daughter. A fund drive netted the $6000 to renovate what was the former Kimball home. On November 11, 1945 the present building was dedicated as a living memorial to the local men and women who served in the Armed Forces during World War II.

The library also outgrew this building, and in 1979, money from the Lewis-Wilmot Fund provided the addition that almost doubled the floor space, providing a separate children's area and a second floor meeting room. The library has been fortunate to have had dedicated staff from the directors down to the high school aides. But it is the personal touch that made the Middleport Free Library special! The library has grown through the efforts of eight directors.

Marjorie Reynolds gave the library its start from 1929-1945; she was followed by her daughter, Doris Bunnell, 1946-1951, who started offering preschool story hour, one of the first programs of its kind in the state; Margaret Blackburn, 1951-1958; Edna Howe, 1958-1975; Katherine Willard, 1975-1976; Irene Drummond, 1976-1978; Marilyn Greenwell, 1978-1999, who met the challenge of keeping a small library in step with technology. She received an Electronic Doorway certificate from the New York State Education Department.

The next director, Melane Shuttleworth, reached out to every age group, offering various craft classes, mother-daughter clubs, and story hour for toddlers, and Friends of the Library. A children's summer reading program has been ongoing for many years.

The Library has a diverse collection of fiction and non-fiction books, reference materials, dozens of magazine titles, as well as large-print books and books on tape, videos and music CDs. As a member of the Nioga System, Middleport is able to inter-loan books from other libraries.

A rededication ceremony in celebration of fifty years in their own home was well attended. Kirby Brown, who dedicated the library in 1945 when he returned from WWII,

147

and Blanche Freeman, a Board Member since 1945, attended the occasion. Senator George Maziarz, Assemblyman David Seaman (who attended Story Hour when he was growing up), and Mayor Donald Piedmont all spoke briefly. The Middleport clergy attended; American Legion Clute-Phillips Post #938 posted the colors.

It was remarked that "as technology advances, the size of the library no longer limits the size of its service. This small village library will continue to provide individual assistance in a warm, friendly atmosphere as it has for the past fifty years." And it has continued to do so!

The list of directors since Mrs. Shuttleworth should include Mrs. Rose Bernard who served from 2010 to 2014. The library now serves the community under its new name of the Royalton Hartland Community Library and the current director is Sonora Miller.
(Image from Patt Fagan)

Schools

It is believed that the first school in the village was the Middleport Academy at what is now at Park Avenue, deeded in 1830 to the Trustees of District #1, Town of Royalton, "and that a school should be erected." It opened in January 1842; the property was sold in 1847. There were several small one-room schools in the vicinity: one in the South Vernon Street area, and a log cabin school on Freeman Road. Torryville just north of the village on N. Hartland Street was District #1, Town of Hartland, and District #4 on Sleeper Street, Town of Hartland, were eventually added to the Union Free School District.

The Middleport Union School on the corner of Park and Vernon, clearly showing the original two story building flanked by the two additions from 1891 and 1898.
(Image from MVH)

The next school was built on the south side of Park Avenue near Vernon Street in about 1846; a one-story frame building was replaced by a two-story stone building in 1870. A wing was added to the west side in about 1891. It was voted to change from the common school district to a Union Free School. In 1898, an addition was made to the east side of the building. Chemical and physical laboratories were improved and a teacher training class was established. While the buildings were not handsome in appearance, they were roomy. The number of students had about doubled from the "common school" to a high school, graduating 136 pupils, with 205 graduating from its training class. The Middleport High School ranked eighth among all the high schools in the state, and just before the fire on February 23, 1910, it had the largest percentage of non-resident pupils statewide.

A newspaper item reported that when the alarm rang, there was only one horse on the street to get the pumper to the fire, so it was pressed into service. The streets were slippery and the horse was encouraged to hurry and after they got to the fire the poor horse died. The owner was paid $15 for his loss. One of the firemen at the scene said that they went to the basement of the Methodist church for coffee and to get warm. Another fireman had a restaurant on Main Street and went to the store to pick up some "spirits" to add to the coffee. And the combination of the bitter cold outside, the heat inside, and the "hot" coffee caused him to fall flat on the floor. The buckles on their jackets were so thickly coated with ice that it had to be chipped off with a hammer; water froze right inside their boots.

Remains of the school building the day after the February 1910 fire.
(Image from MVH)

The fire destroyed every record in the building but the Board of Education and faculty worked vigorously to get the best temporary quarters obtainable. Classes were held in the Firemen's Building, at the Opera House, over some of the Main Street stores, and in the large Kittredge house at the corner of Main and Terry Streets.

Realizing that the school district was too small, the Board began proceedings to enlarge the district and to locate and purchase a site for a new school. At the 1910 annual meeting the members of the Board whose terms expired were unanimously re-elected. After a second vote, the land was purchased on State Street that has been the "old Middleport High School." Ground was broken on July 14th and on September 4th, 1911, the cornerstone was laid - preceded by a HUGE parade.

School Children Corner Stone Laying Sept 4/11

Children lining up to participate in the dedication parade for the new school on State Street in September of 1911. (Image from Wm. Holahan collection)

By a vote of 742 to 194, the plan to merge the Middleport and Gasport School Districts and twenty-six Rural Districts was adopted in 1944, comprising the Royalton-Hartland Central School District. The former Middleport High School with its $125,000 addition in 1939, became part of the present high school. A second vote in 1949 provided for eleven new classrooms, a cafeteria, an industrial arts shop and a gymnasium.

Dignitaries for the parade included past State Senator George F. Thompson, who is driving the car in the parade along Main Street.
(Image from Wm. Holahan collection)

In 1952, a vote approved the purchase of twenty-one acres of land on Route 31 between Orchard Place and Emerson Road for Gasport Elementary School. The Middleport Elementary school was built on land purchased just east of the high school. Both elementary schools opened in the fall of 1958 - a nineteen-classroom building at Middleport and a twenty-five-classroom building at Gasport. Several elementary classes were held in the Ford Garage Building - again the Opera House, and the nearby E & M Building on Vernon Street, until their school was ready.

In the fall of 2006, all K-4 classes were held at the Gasport building; the Middleport elementary building became the Middle School, all grades 5-8; and grades 9-12 were at the high school. 2007 was the first year for the pre-kindergarten program; this was very successful.

The bus garage and all the busses were housed on Route 31 between the two communities. A full history of the Royalton-Hartland Central School District would be a long story in itself, and could be a separate project.

Lewis-Wilmot Fund

The philanthropic trust fund to be known as the Lewis-Wilmot Fund was established under provisions of the will of Mrs. Myrtle Lewis Wilmot, who died in 1974. The income from the trust is to be used for public charitable, educational and worthy purposes in the towns of Royalton and Hartland, including the Village of Middleport. The fund began disbursing monies in 1977; the income is to be used annually. The five trustees of the governing board serve for five year terms; they are appointed by the boards of the Rotary Club, Cataract Lodge F&AM, the Village Board, Royalton-Hartland School Board, and the Middleport Free Library Board.

Mrs. Wilmot was born in Middleport, studied music at the Julliard School of Music in New York City, and taught piano to many local children. She was also an artist, and several of her paintings are on exhibit at the Village Hall and the Library.

Mrs. Wilmot's father, Elgie J. Lewis, was an inventor who operated a machine shop on N. Main Street. Involved with the Ontario Preserving Company, he invented a pineapple paring machine in 1893 that was used locally at the plant, after which they processed carloads of pineapple. This was the first machine that was used extensively in the Hawaiian Islands, as previously the fruit was pared by hand.

Many years later he added coring, slicing and dicing capabilities to the machine. In 1912 he developed a cutting machine used on vegetables that was used for many years by Campbell Soup Company. He also developed the "Lewis Power Can Tester" that was used at BP Co. to test for leaks in newly made tin cans. The tester was also used by Edison Battery Company to test their metal containers for a new electric storage battery that they were making for an electric automobile being produced at the time. Mr. Lewis continued to invent and produce various types of custom machines for many years.

"Myrtie" married Arthur M. Wilmot, son of Dr. Henry A. and Mrs. Wilmot of Middleport, a flying officer with the forerunner of the Army Air Force during WWI. During WWII he was employed by the Curtiss-Wright Airplane Corp. in Buffalo. After the war he was associated with the Studebaker Motor Car Corp. in Buffalo.

Elgie Lewis served his community for a number of years as a member of the Board of Education. Dr. Wilmot served in the same capacity for many years also.

Elgie J. Lewis and his son-in-law
Arthur Wilmot.
(Image from RTH)

Middleport Area Tourism And Beautification Committee

The Middleport Tourism and Beautification ad hoc committee of the Village Board was organized in June 1988 to promote the village as a "friendly community," the term first used on the Rotary Club signs as one enters the village. Eight months later, the ad hoc committee was made a separate committee so that they would have greater freedom in fund raising and event scheduling. In August 1989, they introduced the first Middleport Area Guide Book, which has been updated through their seventh issue. The original committee members were June Peters, Julie Maedl, Janet Lyndaker, and Charles Sheppard.

Through a suggestion box, residents indicated an interest in bringing back Labor Day, and weekend festivities each year since have featured a kiddie parade, a band concert in the park, and food services. Other events have been added at different times. As a non-profit organization, Middleport Area Tourism and Beautification Committee depends on an annual fund drive, concession stand receipts and donations to finance their yearly activities. A 5th Anniversary reception with entertainment was held at the Masonic Hall.

Mr. Gordon Jones, standing in front of his hardware store on Main Street admiring the beautiful flower barrel that was planted by the Middleport Area Tourism and Beautification Committee. (Image from MVH)

The committee coordinates the Labor Day activities, places twenty half barrels of flowers throughout the village, and participates in Niagara County's Festival of Gold daffodil project. Bulletin boards placed on Main Street and on either side of the canal are available for advertising area events. The committee also participates in canal activities.

In 1996, together with the Barge Canal Art Center they designed and purchased the community banners depicting a tree, a bridge and a pleasure boat, that hang from the street light poles in the downtown area. Joining forces again, the project "Time for Middleport" restored the circa-1910 McClintock Loomis clock in 2004. Known as the "Middleport Community Clock," it had graced the corner of the Fenton Hotel for many years. Saved from the wrecking ball in the 1960s when the hotel was demolished , the clock was stored for many years, the Barge Canal Art Center and the Middleport Area Tourism and Beautification Committee raised $20,000 in less than two years. The old village timepiece, illuminated at night, hangs from the second story of the village hall, reminiscent of years gone by.

The committee sponsors a holiday Mitten Tree with HSBC Bank, helps with community caroling in the park, and places decorations and ten lighted trees in the downtown area at Christmas and has sponsored a Christmas Decorating Contest.

The committee helps to foster canal tourism, and is listed in the "Niagara USA Travel Guide." Their Theme: "RING IN THE NEW SPIRIT."

New York Central Railroad

Two routes had been surveyed for the railroad coming into Niagara County in 1841, the Ridge Route and the Canal Route. Both would enter the county at Middleport and continue on to Lewiston and then to Niagara Falls. Sentiment in Hartland was against having the railroad along their ancient highway, with fears of wood-burning engines belching sparks and setting their fields afire or scaring their animals. The Town of Hartland is the only town in the county still having no railroad.

The first locomotives burned wood, and a good sized engine required one to two cords of wood per hour. Farmers on the line contracted to cut and pile wood along the route, and there was public concern for the inroads being made on the wood supply.

The Rochester, Lockport and Niagara Falls Railroad was organized at the close of 1850, and the first train to pass through Middleport was drawn by locomotive #153, the "Niagara" on June 25, 1852. It traveled at the amazing speed of 50 mph. The first scheduled all-passenger train ran on June 30th, drawn by #137, "Willink," and it was saluted at stations along the line with cannons and cheering crowds.

The State charged the railroad the same toll as the canal boats - 2¢ per mile. With the consolidation of ten different lines, the New York Central System was formed in

1853. Heavy traffic required a second track that was started that fall. Within a year, five trains were running both east and west, including an emigrant train. That train was uncomfortable and poorly equipped so that "regular fares" would not be inclined to take advantage of the reduced rates.

Middleport train depot at Vernon Street crossing remained a part of this community until 1965, though trains no longer ran the line for passenger service.
(Image from RTH)

Our depot was built in 1853 between Vernon and Main Streets on the north side of the tracks. Later a freight office was added to handle the large volume of shipping. Mail cars were added in 1852, smoking cars in 1853, and sleepers in 1860. When the big fire burned eighteen buildings on Main Street in 1878, three fire companies from

Lockport arrived by flat car to assist. By 1888 trains were arriving and departing every hour all day long.

In 1859 the first coal burning engine appeared, and in twenty years most of the locomotives burned coal. Oil-burning diesel engines were introduced in 1924. Six-sided, dark green "flagman's shanty" protected the men from the weather. These men were replaced with electronic gates and flashers probably in the late 1950s. There are two of these still around at least until recently, one on Francis Street was probably used as a child's playhouse. Another used as a school bus shelter was given to the Town of Royalton Historical Society, and is now just inside the entrance at Gasport Veterans Park.

Part of the railroad nostalgia was the familiar whistle sounding throughout the countryside, substituting as a time-piece for many residents. The trains ran on Syracuse time which was fifteen minutes faster than Lockport time, and of course varied from city to city. Because the railroads spanned the country, they requested Congress for an organized time system. After years of trying to come up with a satisfactory plan, the Standard Time Act went into effect November 18, 1883.

Passenger train ridership declined as more families owned automobiles and by 1939, only three passenger trains were operating. The last several years that they operated, the two daily trains carried very few passengers. November 25, 1957 marked the end of the New York Central Railroad service from Rochester to Niagara Falls. The passenger train became a victim of the automobile, as the packet boat became a victim of the railroad. Our depot was razed in 1965.

In the spring of 2007, the New York State Department of Transportation proposed closing the Orchard St. railroad crossing and barricading the tracks, supposedly all in the name of "safety." Closing of some crossings would reduce the number of places where train-vehicle accidents could happen, after the increased rail traffic from the ethanol plant at Shelby. On short notice, the village had to hire an expert railroad investigator to argue that the closing would not increase our safety.

A number of residents objected to the move enough to circulate and sign a petition, write letters, and spend a few hours at a meeting at the town hall participating in the public hearing. The testimony of village employees and a presentation by the Chief of the Middleport Fire Department about local fire-fighting operations strengthened the stand of the village.

At the end of 2008, a state administrative judge noted the adamant opposition by the residents as well as the public officials, and rule that the crossing could not be abandoned. It did pay to fight "City Hall."

The Odell House was next to the depot for travelers and has gone through many name changes and owners through the years. Today the building has been abandoned for many years and suffers greatly from neglect. (Image from RTH)

Buffalo, Lockport, And Rochester Trolley

In September 1906 the Buffalo, Lockport and Rochester Railway Co. started laying rails for a high speed electric railway connecting Rochester and Lockport. The route closely paralleled the New York Central Railroad all the way. They used the International Railway Co. tracks from Lockport to Buffalo, Niagara Falls and Olcott.

By the summer of 1908, all of the work was completed except for the section from Middleport to Lockport. Middleport was the obstacle in completing the line as there was a great deal of controversy about having the trolley tracks go through the "Common," the village park.

In May the Courts decided in favor of the Buffalo, Lockport and Rochester Railway Co. and work progressed. Possibly to appease the dissenters, the whole length of Liberty Street was renamed Park Avenue. The tracks entered Middleport at the corner of Alfred Street and Park Avenue, coming down the side of Park Avenue and to the end of Church Street, and then across St. Stephen's Cemetery, though there was difficulty in getting the right-of-way across the cemetery.

Often a Rochester Railway car carried construction materials to Middleport fulfilling requirements of the franchise of running a car over the tracks with specified frequency. Steel poles were used at Middleport, Medina and Brockport; otherwise poles holding the lines were of chestnut set 110 feet apart. The tracks were laid out with easy grades and few curves. Power was distributed through five sub-stations, and station #1 was a half-mile east of Gasport. There were six stops between Shelby Basin, #30, and Reynales Basin, #37.

Three miles west of Middleport at the "long crossing," long mounds of earth carried the elevated trolley bridge of the Buffalo, Lockport and Rochester Railway over the New York Central Railroad tracks. After the trolley ceased operations, this bridge was moved to span the Tonawanda Creek on Rapids Road at "Burdick's Bridge." A substantial quantity of fill was needed in several areas to make a base for the roadbed, and when blasting neared this area the Wickwire Plant and Quarry was opened west of Middleport.

The railway was officially opened from Rochester to Albion on September 4, 1908. On November 17th the Buffalo, Lockport and Rochester Railway was opened to Lockport. Eighteen trolleys ran daily in each direction. Running time between the Rochester and Lockport City lines was one hour and fifty minutes, for the limited; two hours and fifteen minutes for the local runs. The fare from Buffalo to Rochester was $1.10 one way, $2.20 a round trip. In the first ten months of operation, over a million passengers and nearly 850 tons of freight were carried over the line. Freight and express service was offered for shipments of fruit, vegetables and milk, for which the region was noted. The fifty capacity passenger cars contained a smoking compartment, and were painted Pullman green. They travelled at 80 miles per hour, but after a few years the company had the speed reduced.

On June 22, 1909, with several railway officials aboard, a trolley derailed at Kelly Avenue; damage was slight and there was just a minor injury. A picture postcard recorded the event! In 1917, several were injured when an eastbound trolley and a westbound trolley collided at Middleport.

A trolley station opened in August 1914 on the northwest corner of Church and Main Streets, adjoining the Universalist Church sheds. When the post office was built the building was moved to the Kuspa property at the canal gate east of Middleport.

The company was reorganized as the Rochester-Lockport-Buffalo Railway Company in 1919. With the increased number of private automobiles, the Depression and company's financial problems, the trolley went out of business, and the last car ran on April 30, 1931. Highway Route 31 used that right-of-way.

When Main Street was rebuilt in 1995, more tracks were removed; they had been blacktopped over so often, that the street was higher than the curb and water ran into dooryards.

The trolley station on the corner of Main and Church Street. The Universalist Church owned the large building behind the station where they maintained their stalls and a social hall on the second floor.
(Image from RTH)

Theaters

There were theaters in several different locations in Middleport "back when." In 1908, the Opera House was remodeled for the use of the Star Theater. George Fenton, who later owned the hotel, purchased the theater in 1909. Mallison & Root purchased the Star in 1913. When the building was demolished in 2002, "Star Theater" in white paint was still visible on the east side of the building.

Across the street at 3 Vernon, in the old stone building, there was a theater downstairs on the south side of the building. From an inquiry received recently, a Mr. Marrot ran a theater there in 1916 for a time. When I worked in that building in the early 1940s, there were glass slides in a desk drawer of movie star Rudolf Valentino (and I was foolish enough to have left them there!).

The 1940 grand opening flyer announcing the show at
the Star Theater on Main Street
(Image from collection of MVH)

In 1940 Alex and Mary Stornelli, formerly of Medina, opened the Star Theater in the brick building at 26 Main Street, owned by Thomas Ambrose of Albion, on a lease basis; admission was 40¢ for adults and 16¢ for children; eventually they purchased the building. After they opened the Sunset Drive-In they still operated both, but soon sold the Star to Albert Griffith who had managed the Diana Theater in Medina. He was brother of world-renowned movie producer D. W. Griffith. The building was razed in 1975, again because of deteriorating conditions.

In 1950 there were a few drive-ins in the area, and the Stornellis decided to branch out. Their drive-in was built in just ten weeks from idea to opening on August 29, 1950. A 36 foot by 40 foot cement block building on Route 31 housed the projection equipment, restroom, and refreshment booth, with a charcoal fire for doing hot dogs. Three hundred cars could be accommodated, and theirs was the first drive-in movie theater around to provide cars with individual speakers. A children's playground was added between the front ramp and the screen, and the grounds were landscaped. A coffee shop was added and the menu and hours were both expanded.

Middleport post card featuring the Sunset Drive-in as well as the car show on Main Street
(Image from MVH)

The operation became a family affair when their son, Mario and his wife Denise, became involved in the business. Continual improvements brought a wider screen as well as an all automatic projector. A new and larger box office was built and the speaker system was eliminated with the sound being transmitted directly through the vehicles' FM radios.

In 1996, massive renovations were done on the restaurant and projection building, as well as construction of two additional screens, giving the public the choice of three first-run movies. About 230 cars can park around each of the screens, and all are nicely landscaped. Mary had a desire to show more than one movie at a time, and this expansion was done in her memory.

Movies are their business, but Mario is the counterman and Denise is the waitress, and a neater, cleaner restaurant cannot be found any place. There were about 5000 Drive-In Theaters in the 1950s; today there are only about 900 of these operating. We're proud that the Sunset is one of them! They are included in the Don Sander's book, "The American Drive-In Movie Theater."

The Sunset is still family owned and operated with third-generation involvement.

Niagara-Orleans Country Club

The original property on Telegraph Road dates back to 1821 and was mainly a fruit farm. In 1825 the Erie Canal divided the property into four parcels, two on each side of the canal. The two parcels on the south side became the present golf course.

Four Middleport businessmen who were also golf enthusiasts purchased the Behe farm and opened the course in 1931 - Dan Connolly, Frank Tracey, Jeremiah Tracey and Roy L. Wheeler. The fairways of about 100 acres were seeded with a grain drill. The foundation of the brick house that had been planned to be the clubhouse and burned to the ground the winter before, can still be seen in the parking lot behind the ninth green. The original barn had no floors, but was rushed into service as the clubhouse. Middleport was the first community in the area to have a full-sized public course.

After previous ownership by Roy Emendorf, Chase and Albert Brown, Ralph Stonehouse (the first person to tee off at the first Masters Tournament), and Car-de-Lew Enterprises, the property was purchased by Dan Graney in 1978. He and Dudley Jackson are the club pros. The clubhouse and golf course have been remodeled; irrigation was installed in 1992. Today the beautiful, scenic, par 71, eighteen-hole course measures over 6000 yards.

The clubhouse burned in 2002, and was rebuilt in the fall of 2003. Banquet facilities seating up to 150 are available for sit down meals, station buffets and outing barbeques.

The Niagara-Orleans Country Club is a member of the United States, the New York State, the Buffalo District, and the National Golf Associations.

The barn which housed the original Niagara-Orleans Country Club.
(Image from RTH)

Our Opera House

The early opera houses were the major centers for entertainment and activity for their communities. The first one here was Compton's Opera House at what is now 26 Main Street. It burned in 1876.

The brick Opera House that we have known at 10 State Street was built in 1878 at a cost of $15,000 by James P. Compton, owner of a hardware store. He gave notice in the May 1876 newspaper that he was erecting a new block and wanted all outstanding accounts settled as soon as possible.

In 1885 it was known as the VanDyke Opera House, owned by Robert Davison and managed by J. VanDyke. More dressing rooms were added, more chairs purchased, and the box office was relocated at the head of the stairs. From an early postcard picture, it looks as though the box office might have been a small "room" located on ground level at the east front corner of the building.

Crowd of folks ready to enjoy a performance at the Opera House on State Street.
(Image from MVH)

Max Harpuder moved to Middleport from Wilcox, PA, in 1895 to open a clothing business, and the Opera House was the only building available for purchase. He had his business on the street level, and managed the music house for two years, featuring the Guy Brothers Minstrel Shows and other troupes, including medicine shows. In 1897 he moved his clothing business to the Linus Spalding store at 25 Main Street, where he then remained.

Many parties were held at the Opera House; Mrs. Ella Taylor Bennett directed many plays as she had a wide experience in theater before coming to Middleport. A skating rink was opened in 1908, skating two nights per week with a seven-piece orchestra furnishing music; 15¢ included rental of skates. The Opera House was remodeled for the use of the Star Theater; George Fenton purchased the theater in 1909; Mallison & Root purchased the Star in 1913. A series of dances were held there in 1914, and a banquet was held in honor of George F. Thompson, possibly when he was elected New York State Senator in 1914. In 1924 the High School's Senior Ball was held there.

Sears Motor Sales in the Opera House block in the 1920s.
(Image from RTH)

Automobile agencies used the building from the time of the Sears Motor Sales in the early 1920s, and dances were held upstairs at "Sears Hall." When Hollinger & Shaw purchased the building in 1932 they displayed their new autos in the showroom on the first floor, and warehoused their used autos in the upstairs. A wide, steep ramp came down to the street level, and once when an employee was bringing a car down, its brakes failed. It shot straight across the street, into a dooryard, between a tree and a telephone pole - no damage done! No traffic coming!! Upstairs space was used for school classrooms in 1890 before the second addition to the Park Avenue school, and again in 1910 after that school burned. In the 1950s the showroom housed two elementary grades for the Royalton-Hartland Central School System while the new elementary school was being built.

The last business there was Village Auto Parts from 1972 and for about 20 years. Owned by a non-resident who subsequently had died, the old Opera House was demolished in 2002 because of a long-time deteriorating and dangerous condition. And at that time "Star Theater" in white paint was still visible on the east side of the building.

The Middleport Band

The first reference we have seen to the Middleport Band was from a Lockport newspaper of August 1840. At a Democratic Rally for President Martin VanBuren at Lockport, the Town of Royalton procession was accompanied by an "excellent band of music from Middleport." In the September 1841 Niagara Courier it mentioned that the Middleport Band headed the procession in connection with a temperance rally at Lockport.

Few pictures have been found of the Coronet Band but we know they were active starting in the 1840s to the turn of the century.
(Image from Wm. Holahan files)

We don't read of activity again for about twenty years when the Middleport Cornet Band was organized with sixteen members: President, George A. Depew; Secretary, Burt H. Philleo; Charles H. Hammond, Frank Page, Wm. E. Vincent, Frank Sterritt, Warren Pearce, Walter Seaman, Frank Wittman, Joseph A. Duquette, George B. Hinman, A. Howard Depew, Charles R. Richardson, Dean Root, Fred Howland and B. Frank Pencille. There was indebtedness to John Benson, a local man, of $170 for new instruments.

Over the years the Middleport Band was referred to as the Brass Band and the Saxophone Horn Band. The Band played at a "pole raising" at Gasport in 1860 attended by about 2000 people, when streamers with the names of Lincoln and Hamlin were run up the 140-foot pole. In September 1861 at a meeting to raise volunteers for the Cavalry Company being organized in the area, "the Middleport Brass Band volunteered their services and enlivened the meeting with their soul, stirring patriotic music at the Pierce Hotel." Five young men responded to the call and a bounty of $25 each was offered by the citizens to be paid when they were mustered into service.

In 1872 the Middleport Saxophone Horn Band met the delegation arriving by train for the Universalist Church Picnic.

From 1889 they were again the Cornet Band, leading the Decoration Day parade, held a skating party, a Thanksgiving dance and turkey dinner at the Opera House, and a "very pleasant" dance in the new building at the canning factory. They were reinforced with several new members. A picture taken around 1900 identifies members Stephen Sherman, Walter Vary, John Mufford, Everett

Pearce, partner in his father's harness shop; Mr. Howell, Charles R. Richardson, later a local funeral director; Fred Clawson, and Charles Hammond, later band director at the Middleport High School.

On January 2, 1901, the Middleport Cornet Band led the New Century Parade through the village at midnight. In June 1902 the band was reorganized but we have seen no later information about it.

Baseball

Baseball has been played in this country for about 200 years. The first we heard about baseball in Middleport was an 1876 village ordinance prohibiting ball-playing on public streets, and ball-playing was forbidden within the corporation limits on Sundays.

A baseball club with nine members, and complete with uniforms, was formed in 1888, playing on "Miller Grounds" at the south end of the present Kelly Avenue. That summer they were undefeated; when playing at Albion they traveled in the Wicks Brothers' "Steamer." The next year the club engaged the Slayton Full Orchestra for their Grand Harvest Festival at Compton's new hay barn, with a game in the afternoon.

By 1928 the Middleport "Superiors" were playing at Knapp Field and drawing the largest crowds of all the eight counties where they played. They "easily were the championship semi-professional baseball team in Western New York." They played Saturday afternoon and Sunday games, with twilight games squeezed in.

Baseball was popular in the Village of Middleport but not on public streets and certainly not on Sunday. (Image from MVH)

The aim of the Superiors was not necessarily to win games, but to develop amateur athletics and clean sport among the youth of the village. The coach and manager were coaching the boys of the high school to give them training that would make them available for an all-home semi-professional team as the years passed.

The Knapp Field Association was incorporated in 1929 so that recreational facilities would be available locally. For three years, the field on the north side of Route 31 was loaned to the association by the Niagara Sprayer & Chemical Co. There were three well drained tennis courts; a baseball diamond with benches, dugouts and backstops; three well laid out lanes for horseshoes, and a completely furnished trap shoot layout used by Niagara-Orleans Rod & Gun Club.

In 1936, Middleport had a town team in the Eastern Suburban League. The Sunday afternoon routine for many was to follow the team to wherever they were playing. At this time, the home games were played in the field that is now Hammond Parkway.

First Universalist Church

The first time that the doctrine of the Universalist Church was preached here, the service was held in the little frame schoolhouse at Ewing's Corners. From that meeting in 1833 until 1841, the Universalist society depended on the circuit preachers to hold their meetings in homes, and often in the little brick school at what is now 5 Park Avenue.

The beautiful cobblestone Universalist Church, corner of Main and Church, was organized in 1841 and built by the congregation who collected the round stones from Lake Ontario.
(Image from postcard in MVH collection)

These early Universalists met with a great deal of opposition from the Methodists, and the Presbyterians especially, who tried to break up their meetings, sometimes resorting to sticks and stones. Their philosophy was attacked, and the members were called heretics.

On April 6, 1841, a small group of about twenty people were officially organized into the First Universalist Association of Middleport, and received fellowship in the Niagara Association. Elijah Mather was named Moderator; Alden S. Baker, Clerk; and John Craig, Dudley Watson and Linus Spalding, Trustees. During their first year, the building of their cobblestone church was undertaken, on land donated to the Association by John Craig, a prominent businessman.

For a long time Mrs. Alden S. Baker was the only woman who would, or did, attend their meetings, and for a long time was the only female member of the Society.

The stones used in construction of the church were hauled from Lake Ontario, and entire families of the congregation would spend sixteen-hour days gathering them. They would leave their homes about 4:00am with their wagon and team of oxen; the women and children would gather the smooth egg-shaped stones, and the men would sort them according to size. Two or three carts could be filled with stones in one day.

Emery J. Smith, great-great-grandfather of Helen Moore Walso, an early resident of Middleport, specialized in the cobblestone architecture. He and Mary Ann Russell were the first couple to be married in the church, as soon as temporary flooring was installed.

Before the actual building could begin, lime had to be burned for making the mortar. An experienced stonemason could lay up about eighteen inches of wall on all sides in one day, but the walls then had to dry for three weeks before another eighteen inches could be applied.

This church was a replica of another Universalist Church at Chittenden, Vermont. In cobblestone circles, this church is always referred to as an excellent example of cobblestone architecture. When completed, it was appraised for $5000. The 1842 bell that still hangs in the steeple, the first bell in the village, is said to weigh 1,000 pounds. The Sunday school was established in 1865-66. The brick house at 43 State Street was built as the parsonage in 1878.

Their Social Hall stood along Church Street on part of the land now occupied by the post office, and for many years, it was the scene of public dinners, parties and dances. It was a two-story wooden building, with horse sheds below and the social hall above, probably built about 1892. The stained glass windows were added in 1915, and thirty years ago were valued at $100,000.

In 1925, the Sheldon home next to the church was purchased to be used as the parsonage, and the new $30,000 Parish Hall, built between the church and the parsonage, replaced the old Social Hall. The new hall was dedicated in February 1928, and also became the scene of many community activities.

In 1976 the church was listed as a Historical Landmark. That year, the congregation sent their minister,

The Rev. Sydney Mayell, on an all day tour of the Holy Land. Rev. Mayell died in 1980 and the church was kept open by the church members and guest speakers until Rev. Charles O. Boseck assumed the pastorate in 1986. An extensive project of repainting the cobblestone part of the structure was completed that year.

In 1994 new musicians robes were given in memory of Bernice Guild, a sixty-nine-year member of the church and a long time choir member.

The Organ Historical Society visited our area in 2004 and a recital was held in this church with J. R. Daniels playing the 1902 Carol Barckoff organ. This was the first church in the village to have an organ. This recital was also held at the Fundamental Baptist Church. Rev. Paul Letiecq served the congregation as its last minister.

Holy Cross Lutheran Church

After several exploratory meetings, the first service of the Holy Cross Lutheran Church, Missouri Synod was held in the former Star Theater building, 26 Main Street, on January 3, 1954, with sixty-five people attending the service. The congregation was formed on January 17, 1954.

Rev. Hilbert J. Huth, who was pastor of Wolcottsville St. Michael's Lutheran Church, conducted the service and led the congregation until the installation of Rev. Otto F. Strothmann as resident pastor on August 19, 1956. Rev. Strothmann served until December 8, 1963. A house at 42 S. Vernon Street was purchased from Robert Wright to serve as the parish house.

Land on Route 31 was purchased from Christopher Poehlmann, and ground was broken for the new church on August 28, 1955; the cornerstone was laid on June 14, 1959. Services were held in the completed basement until the church building was dedicated on April 3, 1960.

Rev. Gerald J. Grimm was installed as the second pastor in July 1964, serving until February 1982. The mortgage burning was held on April 1, 1979 in conjunction with the 25th Anniversary Celebration.

*View of the altar inside the old Star Theater building
where the Lutheran congregation held services until
the completion of their new church on Route 31.
Services were led by Rev. Hilbert Huth from
St. Michael's in Wolcottsville.
(Image from the Medina Journal Register courtesy of
Mrs. Melane Shuttleworth)*

Rev. Barlow of the Medina Trinity Lutheran Church was the interim pastor with a dual charge, until Rev. William A. Dietche, 1983-1987. The addition in 1988 provided ground level handicapped accessible rest rooms and a new pastor's office. Rev. Dennis Krueger served from 1989, followed by Rev. David Triplett in 1994.

Holy Cross became a member of the new Lutheran Brotherhood's Fraternal Division in 1987, Thirteen Communities Branch #8546, established on the Niagara Frontier.

Methodist Episcopal Church, The Methodist Church, United Methodist Church

Methodism first came to this area via the Ridgeway Circuit starting in 1816. The Methodist society was organized at Middleport on April 18, 1827. Rev. John Copeland, Preacher in Charge of the Circuit, purchased the land on which the church was built, presided at the election of Trustees and gave a Warranty Deed to the lot on the south side of Park Avenue at Main Street. Building of the two-story frame structure began at once.

Middleport was part of a seven-member circuit including churches from Royalton Center to Orangeport and Hartland. In 1843 the circuit was divided and the new Middleport circuit included six churches from Quaker Road to County Line. In 1860 Middleport was a single charge.

The present church at Park Avenue and Vernon is built on the site of the old Vernon House hotel, and the bricks were made at the J. A. Parker brick yard on the east side of Stone Road near Ridge Road. The total cost of $13,424.64 included pews and the stained glass windows. Storm windows were eventually put on to protect the windows, costing $580 at the time, and now worth much, much more!!

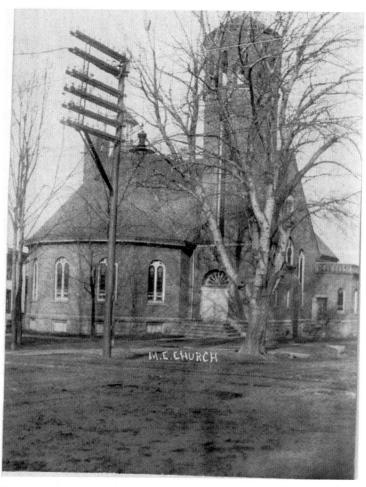

The new Methodist Church was dedicated in 1900 at what had been the site of the old Vernon House, earlier destroyed by a fire.
(Image from RHCL)

The church was dedicated on March 15, 1900. The old church was sold and used as a plumbing supply warehouse; a fire next door in the high school at Park

Avenue and Vernon on February 23, 1910 burned both buildings to the ground.

The first large purchase was the organ in 1907 at a cost of $2000, which was paid for in four years. It was electrified, chimes were added, and it was relocated from the center of the choir loft in 1955. The first major improvement was in 1911 when the peaked, circular roof was put on the south half of the building. A picture shows the original roof to be flat, and records indicated that there were constant leaks.

Proceeds from the two-day flower show enlarged the dining room and kitchen when village water was available in 1913, followed by steam heating the next year. Nothing more was done to the kitchen until the big fund drive of 1973, at the "suggestion" of the Health Department. And nothing more has been done since until new kitchen cupboards this year.

The green carpeting with the large gold tulips, purchased by the Ladies' Aid in 1917, was strip-carpet from the Pullman Railroad Company; plain green carpet was installed in 1955; the present red carpet was given anonymously in 1996.

In preparation for the 100th Anniversary celebration, doors were put on the basement opening; the wooden steps were replaced with concrete steps with a canopy. Heavy front doors replaced with plain barn-door type ones and were fitted with locks! The newer red doors came anonymously in the 1980s; the present doors with crash bars were given in memory of Donald Coe.

During WWII when the Methodist Church was without a minister for nine months, the Universalist minister conducted joint services there, giving regular services and saving fuel for them, until a discharged Army Chaplain came to the Methodist Church. The Methodist Church had a very close relationship with the Universalist Church for ninety years beginning in about 1880.

By 1972, the entire tower had been removed from the structure.
(Image from RHCL)

The structural changes are the most obvious, and most of the unique features have been lost. First, on the upper section of the tower, the two large windows on either side of the building were filled in; then the "walls of ivy" were removed when the ivy's' toehold loosened the brick. In 1972, the whole tower was removed. An amplifier that had played chime music every Sunday before church and every night at 6 p.m. for twenty-five years met its demise for lack of enthusiasm, and now would have lost its home in the tower.

The Methodist Church was blessed with growing pains, and the educational building was added in 1960, the plan submitted by a lady from the congregation. The Philathea Society's memorial pine trees grew too large and were scrawny since the 1950s, and were replaced with the memorial flowerbed, which now grows into a large, live cross.

At the 150th Anniversary Celebration, a full day of activity included District Superintendent Charles Aldrich preaching at the morning service, with Pastor Edward C. Hannay and former pastors participating. Following that, a buffet dinner was served to 140 people. Bishop Joseph Yaekel gave an address during the afternoon program.

Pastor Emeritus Alfred L. Underhill, who served for an unprecedented nineteen years, was presented with the original sketch of the church done by local artist Richard Heim that was produced on the souvenir plates. Frank House reminisced about the years that his father, Fred C. House, served the church in the 1920s.

As part of the yearlong 165th Anniversary Celebration a special service and dinner was held. Rev.

Calvin W. Babcock shared some of his memories of growing up in the parsonage when his father, John Wesley Babcock was pastor, and of the years when he recently served. Rev. Everett Hendrickson served for sixteen years, and Diane is remembered for the Valentine family of classic stuffed teddy bears that she made. He was followed by Rev. Andrew Pollock with three young children, who remained on the charge for eleven years, and chose a picnic at Rotary Park for the "get acquainted" time. He was ordained while here, the "first ever," and the Pastor-Parish Relations committee noted the time with an all out "party." He was chaplain of the Middleport Fire Department and worked with Tri-Town Ambulance.

Rev. Karen S. Grinnell is the first woman to serve this congregation soon after coming here in 2006 just after she was ordained.

In 2008 the sanctuary was repainted, the outside brick was repainted, and the stained glass windows were completely refurbished.

Presbyterian Church

The Presbyterian Church was organized June 11, 1833, and they suffered through ups and downs all during their existence.

Their first church was on Cemetery Street, for in 1865 the Episcopal Church rented the property in which had not been occupied for several years. In 1868, they decided to revive their congregation, and Trinity built their own church.

The second Presbyterian Church was at the site of the present Roman Catholic Church, and was sold to St. Stephen's in 1875.

On January 3, 1889, their new church at the corner of Park Avenue and Vernon Street was dedicated; it was built by veteran church builder Hon. Wm. Morgan of Somerset. A newspaper item reported that the resignation of Rev. Wm. H. Poole, in October 1926, closed the church. That must have been temporary, for in February 1933, "the death of Rev. George A Jackson, pastor of the Middleport Presbyterian Church" was reported.

The church was sold to St. Stephen's Church in 1933 and is now their Parish Hall.

This was the third church the Presbyterian congregation used for worship and is now the parish hall for St. Stephen's. It is located on the corner of Vernon and Park Avenue
(Image from RHCL)

St. Stephen's Roman Catholic Church

The first mass for the Middleport congregation of the Roman Catholic Church was held in 1854 at the home of Timothy Morrissey on North Hartland Street, by the Rev. Martin O'Connor, pastor of St. Mary's church, Medina. Prior to this, the few Catholic people residing here attended church in Medina.

The following year the bishop at Buffalo visited Middleport and purchased a 132 foot by 82 foot lot on Cemetery Street, and a small frame building was erected and served as their place of worship for nearly twenty years, with Medina pastors continuing to care for the congregation.

In 1875, the Presbyterian Church fronting on Vernon Street, and adjoining the original property, was purchased for $1700, and this served the steadily growing congregation until the erection of the present church. This church was built of Medina sandstone on practically the same site and was dedicated August 8, 1909. The organ was a benefaction of Andrew Carnegie.

The first Catholic Church was purchased from the Presbyterians and the adjoining property became the rectory.
(Image from postcard donated by Mrs. Grace Darroch)

St. Stephen's operated as a "mission" until 1877, when it was established as a parish. The first resident pastor was Rev. J. C. O'Reilly in 1878, who was also in charge of St. Mary's Mission at Gasport, an arrangement that was continued until 1970. The rectory was built about 1882.

The Catholics of Middleport buried their dead at Medina or Somerset until 1888 when St. Stephen's purchased their own cemetery on Watson Avenue. The sale of the right-of-way through the cemetery to the Buffalo-Lockport-Rochester Electric Company helped to raise the $15,000 to begin building of the new church.

St. Stephen's Church was built on the same property using Medina sandstone and dedicated in 1909. (Image from RHCL)

Thirty-five sons of the little parish went into the service in and all during the WWI the St. Stephen's War Relief Association, made up exclusively of men from the parish, kept in touch with every serviceman from Middleport and vicinity, irrespective of religious affiliation.

The church bell was given by Joanna Lahey in memory of her husband and sons in 1919. When the church had a sexton the bell was tolled before each mass. By the end of 1920 the church was free from debt. The Presbyterian Church at Park and Vernon was purchased in 1933, and is their Parish Hall.

In honor of the 125th anniversary, the interior of the church was completely remodeled and an outdoor shrine to Mary was dedicated by the parishioners of former pastor

Father Daniel Duggan, who had died at the rectory in 1975. In 1992 a more extensive redecoration was undertaken, including new carpeting and rearranging a few rows of pews to improve the flow of traffic during Liturgy.

This is the original interior of the old church, which has undergone several remodeling efforts by the congregation. (Image from RHCL)

Upon the retirement of Father Samuel Faiola, St. Stephen's again became a linked parish with St. Mary's at Gasport. Father James Streng served both parishes. Sister Michele Jackson became Director of Religious Education, revitalizing the educational programs for young people of grade and high school ages, before she retired in 1999.

Three members of the parish have been ordained priests. They are: Father Andrew Hartigan, Father James Bray, and Father Daniel Campbell, SJ. Two parish members became sisters: Sister Anne Hoyer, OSF, and Sister Kathleen Britt, SSJ. In 1978, parishioner Nelson Darroch was ordained to the order of permanent deacon and was a member of the first class of men prepared and called to the order.

In 2001, four high school seniors were awarded college scholarships through a fund established by Judith Schwann.

The Eastern Niagara Vicariate had the challenge of placing five priests to cover thirteen parishes. Diocese downsizing was driven by the shortage of priests and the loss of church-going population especially in the larger cities, which didn't exempt the rural churches from reorganization, even though their attendance remained steady.

Physical reorganization reflected practical concerns, including age, condition and location of the individual churches, and the seating and parking facilities. Some parishioners felt that dividing the Gasport, Middleport and Barker parishes was not in their best interests. Middleport and Gasport have shared a priest for ten years and have been closely allied for many years. Their successful youth group is made up of people already attending the same public school. Barker has joined them for some time on missionary and social functions.

The plan adopted by the Commission on Journey of Faith and Grace voted to merge St. Stephen's Parish and St. Mary's Parish of Medina, using both sites and sharing a priest, taking effect in 2008.

The new name adopted by both parishes is Holy Trinity Parish. The Rev. Dan Fawls is pastor; the Parish rectory is at Medina.

Trinity Episcopal Church,
New Hope Missionary Baptist Church,
Middleport Fundamental Baptist Church

Beginning in July 1864, evening Episcopal Church services were held in Middleport with area rectors presiding at "Middleport Mission." There were no church families to form a nucleus, but a good congregation was soon built; the old Presbyterian Church on Cemetery Street that had been vacant for several years was secured for the services. A parish was incorporated under the name of Trinity Church on August 1, 1866.

Episcopal services were held in this building on Main Street, which held its groundbreaking in 1859. (Image from RHCL)

The Presbyterians decided to resume services in their building, and in the spring of 1859, ground was broken for an Episcopal Church on a lot donated by parishioner Mrs. Avery S. DeLano at 56 Main Street. The cornerstone was laid on May 31st for the gothic style brick church, and though the building was not completed, the first service could be held in the basement on Christmas Day. The church was completed by 1872, at a cost of $11,000.

From 1875-77, the church owned a rectory. Another rectory was built on South Vernon Street in 1900 on a lot donated by Warden George W. Eddy; this house was sold in 1909. In January 1884, a fire destroyed the church, and it was rebuilt and reconstructed on November 1st.

Electricity was installed in the church in 1902, and a contract was made with the Village of Middleport to place an electric striking apparatus in the bell tower for fire alarm purposes, at a rental of $25 per year. This was continued for several years.

The pipe organ was installed in 1906, half the cost of $1200 given by philanthropist Andrew Carnegie.

1929 was a milestone in the history of Trinity Parish, as it was voted to change from an Independent Parish to a Dependent Parish, and the title of the church property was transferred to the "Diocesan Board of Trustees."

The church was closed for the winters of 1977-78 and 1978-79 to conserve on heating costs, and with only about twenty communicant families, it was voted to close the church in 1979.

On June 21, 1981, the New Hope Baptist congregation held their first service in the former Trinity Episcopal Church in anticipation of purchasing the property. Under the leadership of Rev. Robert Long as pastor and Rev. Richard Hollow as assistant pastor the black congregation had been worshipping at the Masonic Temple of Medina. After a relatively short time they relinquished use of the building and it was sold.

The first service of the Middleport Fundamental Baptist Church was held on Sunday January 11, 1984 with Rev. David L. Houseman, pastor. The church was rented for one year with the option to buy and it was purchased in March 1985.

Glass storm doors were installed and the following year extensive remodeling was done in the downstairs area. The new baptistery was dedicated in 1992. A mortgage burning service was held in 1994.

In 2004 the Organ Historical Society visited our area, and two concerts were held in Middleport and one at Wolcottsville. A recital on the 1906 Carol Barckoff organ was performed by Kristin Farmer in this church.

The church has hosted a free clothes closet for several years on the first Saturday of the month, with good donated items available for the taking.

The nucleus of the congregation was a bible study group organized in October 1983, meeting in different homes in the area. In a short time they decided to organize as a parish.

Middleport Area Clergy And Churches Association, Middleport Community Choir

The pastors of the village churches began meeting in 1998 as the Middleport Area Clergy & Churches Association. Together they have hosted youth events, concerts, and the National Day of Prayer.

At the National Day of Prayer, a short service is held at the flag pole in Veterans Park at noon, followed by a luncheon at the Fire Hall. Salads, sandwiches and desserts are furnished by the four churches: the Middleport Lutheran, United Methodist, Universalist and Catholic churches. The $3 donation benefits the Tri-Town Food Pantry.

Each church had provided emergency food for some time, but their efforts were consolidated in 1993. The Middleport area food pantry is housed in St. Stephen's Parish Hall, the former Presbyterian Church. The first year of the Middleport Postal workers annual collection provided 500 pounds of food in 1993; in 1999, their collection was 1500 pounds. In 1999, Middleport Area Clergy And Churches Association also hosted the visitors from St. Andrew's Brass Ensemble from Lübbecke, Germany.

The visit by our German friends marked the beginning of the Middleport Community Choirs - a new way for people of faith to fellowship with each other. There are two choirs: the singing group, the Middleport Community Choirs, and the hand bell choir, the "Middleport Bell Tones." The choirs are made up of members of the four churches.

The Middleport Community Choirs had its beginning when members of the Middleport area parish choirs performed together for special church services. In early 1999 a special effort was made to form a choir that would perform in concert with the visiting St. Andrews Brass Ensemble. Both groups also performed at an Easter Sunrise service. An offering collected at the concert realized $1100 for the food pantry that aids families in need.

German visitors from Lübbecke performed in the Common in 2005 on their second trip to Middleport. The exchange continues to the present day with strong bonds of friendship between the two communities.
(Image from MVH)

While in Middleport, our German friends stayed with members of the Middleport Community Choirs, and they visited several nearby sites to learn about our area. Before leaving, the Brass Ensemble extended an invitation to visit them in 2001. September 12-26 were dates for the trip, but the events of 9/11 caused cancellation of travel plans.

The Bell Tones began practicing for their Germany trip in 2000. A number of the ringers had been playing at services at the United Methodist church for a time, but many of them were brand new.

In an effort to assist victims of the 9/11 attacks, a series of local concerts collected more than $4000 for disaster relief. Presently the choirs perform at local civic and religious functions. The Germany trip was rescheduled for September 2002.

The St. Andrew's Brass Ensemble made their second visit to Middleport in August 2005; the Middleport Community Choirs returned to Lübbecke in July 2008.

Doctors

The first resident physician in the Town of Royalton is said to have been Dr. Benjamin H. Packard, who settled a mile southwest of Middleport, now the Manor Lane area, in 1817. He was one of three Commissioners of Common Schools after the Town of Royalton was formed, and in 1824 was on a committee of three to solicit subscriptions for the "Greek Cause," during the time of their revolution. After moving to Michigan in 1827, he and two minister friends became founders of Albion College at Albion, Michigan, now a Methodist-related co-ed college.

1823 - Dr. Eli Hurd came to the Middleport area; he died 1860.

1830 - Dr. Jacob Chatterton followed Dr. Packard, and stayed for some time.

1834 - W. H. Bessoc, MD. "His office is a few rods east of the Methodist meeting house; "will devote particular attention to diseases of the eye."

1847 - Dr. Wm. McKinnon of Albion began his practice in Middleport; returned to Albion 1852.

1860 - F. S. Taylor, physician and surgeon.

1862 - James S. Wilkin, physician, had located at Middleport and begun the practice of medicine. He graduated from Buffalo Medical School in 1866.

1863 - Electus Cole, physician and surgeon, office and residence at the Vernon House in 1874. Office above Taylor Drug Store in 1880. Killed in a runaway accident in 1885.

1863 - Richard W. Briggs, magnetic physician, electric treatment a specialty in 1874. Died about 1889, age 85.

1871 - Cassius W. Gould, physician, surgeon, and druggist on State Street in 1875. Coroner 1880. He moved to Chicago in 1885 as a representative in the Gould Coupler Company.

1874 - Edward L. Downey, physician and surgeon, office over bank. "Electric physician," using both conventional and herbal medicines, until 1891.

1876 - Charles M. Garlock, physician, office at residence on State Street. Moved to Rochester 1888, later to New York City.

1883 - John B. Hoyer, physician and surgeon at 5 Park Avenue in 1891. Served two terms as mayor; died in 1914.

1877 - Henry A. Wilmot attended medical college and began the practice of medicine on Main Street corner of Mechanic. Purchased the house of Dr. Garlock when he left

Middleport. Came here in 1873 as principal of the public school; first president of the Union Free School Board, 1891.

1888 - C. B. LeVan of Middleport graduated from Buffalo Medical College "and will hang his shingle here," but soon he was resident physician at Quarantine Hospital, Buffalo.

1888 - George Jackson, doctor at Wolcottsville.

1889 - Prof. M. L. Failing fitting glasses at the Rich Hotel. Evening fittings by gas light.

1891 - L. C. Broughton, physician, Main Street.

1891 - C. T. Brown, physician and druggist, Main Street.

1891 - Mrs. Helen M. Robertson, homeopathic physician, our first local female doctor. Began medical school at the age of fifty and practiced at the family home, 33 State Street, for 35 years until shortly before her death. Her daughter, Helen Evans Robertson, graduated from the same college in 1903, practiced in Winnetka, Illinois.

1900 - T. Arnold Addy came from Canada. About two years later he was thrown from his bicycle and fractured his shoulder and both arms. He rode his bicycle or walked even on country calls; he never did drive a car. In his older years, a younger businessman would drive him on long house calls.

1901 - Dr. Sawyer, formerly of Middleport, was killed in his office in Vermont when lightning struck a pole a half mile away while he was on the telephone.

1904 - L. A. Damon; after he was married in 1914 they lived in the home owned by the Dr. Hoyer estate until it was purchased by the Methodist Church in 1916.

1909 - J. Jay Walker, osteopathic physician opens his office here. Later went to Medina.

1914 - Ernest Herbert Purvis, physician and surgeon; eye, ear, nose, and throat specialist. In 1933, Dr. and Mrs. Purvis moved from State Street to Lockport.

1924 - Robert A. Munson, son of Dr. Ed. Munson, Medina, opened an office here. Served with the US Navy Medical Corp in WWI. Served as Health Officer, Middleport Office, 17 State Street. Died 1940.

1927 - Clayton H. Thomas came to Middleport; Head-EENT (eye, ear, nose, and throat) specialist serving Middleport and Medina. In 1950, he moved to Center Street, Medina. Born in Ontario, Canada, he served with a Tank Battalion in WWI. Graduated from University of Toronto, specialized in Buffalo. Died in 1985.

1936 - Kent D. Williams, physician and surgeon, was school physician for nearly thirty-five years. Named to Fellowship in the College of Surgeons 1943. Was Chief of surgery at Medina Memorial Hospital for 25 years, and Dean of Medicine there. Was a founding member of the

American Board of Abdominal Surgery. He retired to
Florida in 1975; died in 1986.

*Items belonging to the practice of Dr.
Kent Williams, who practiced general
medicine from his home on the corner of
State Street and Maple Ave.
(Image from MVH)*

1941 - Hans Lowenstein practiced here for forty
years. Born in Germany, he served with the German Field
Artillery in WWI. Practiced obstetrics and gynecology in
Berlin until 1938 when he was interned in a Nazi
Concentration Camp. His wife worked to secure his release,
and after a time in England came to the United States. Here,
he had to locate in a community of less than 3,000; after
getting his New York State license he came to Middleport.
He retired for health reasons in 1981; died 1982.

1955 - E. Scott Francis served in the US Army European Theater of Operations, 1944-1946. He graduated from Western Reserve Medical School, Cleveland and was on the staff at Medina Memorial Hospital. Died in 1962 after a short illness.

1963 - Albert G. Connette began practice in Lockport 1955, then he came to 53 State Street.

1972 - Abraham M. Saludo, internal medicine and cardiology, graduated from medical school in the Philippines. Lived at 22 Park Avenue and practiced out of Medina Hospital.

1975 - Dicky Oswari graduated from the University of Indonesia, interned in New York City with training in pediatrics. He opened his first private practice at 19 Main Street.

1975 - Surinder S. Bath arrived to join new physicians on Medina Memorial Hospital staff. Lives at 14 Locust Drive; his office is at 911 West Center Street, Medina.

1978 - D. Douglas Gilbert returned to his home town, and opened a practice at 3 N. Main Street. Moved to Erie, PA, 1980, accepting a fellowship in further surgery after completing osteopathic medicine and surgery.

1982 - David D. Stahl returned to his hometown to open an office at 6 State Street for the practice of internal medicine. He built an office at 21 N. Main Street; Deborah White joined him in 1990 - she was killed in an auto accident in 1999. Physician Assistant Ronal Miller is associated with the office. Medina Health Care System also has a Diagnostic Center also at 21 North Main Street.

1993 - Thomas J. Madejski, a specialist in internal medicine from Williamson, NY, opened Lake Plains Medical Associates at 9916 Rochester Rd., Middleport. He moved his office to 100 Ohio Street, Medina.

1995 - Patricia Mayhew, a massage therapist, opened "A Kneaded Touch" at her home at 77 State Street. She died in 2004.

1997 - Lockport Pediatric Associates opened at 23 N. Main Street. Their office has since moved to Lockport.

1998 - A second location of the Medina Woman's Health Center opened at 23 N. Main Street.

1998 - Terrance L. Klinetob, earlier a resident of Middleport opened an office for physical therapy at 149 Telegraph Road after several years of hospital-based physical therapy. He is now located at 23 N. Main Street.

1992 - Timothy L. Speciale, a former physical therapist at Medina Memorial Hospital, lived in Middleport before entering Philadelphia College of Osteopathic Medicine. He opened his office in Tonawanda specializing in nonsurgical orthopedics and sports medicine.

A newspaper item from 1936 reported a birth at Owen's Private Hospital at 39 Francis Street, the maternity hospital of Mrs. Lydia Owen. From 1939-1941 it was listed as Vinehurst Nursing Home on Francis Street, owned by Mrs. Jane Cramer Burke. About forty babies a year began their lives there.

Dentists

1881 - J. M. Card - Opera Block 1885.

1885- L. Balcom - Main Street.

1887 - Almon Dewhirst opened his office here, over different Main St. stores until 1931.

1933 - Edward A. Roberts of Lockport opened in the office of Dr. Dewhirst.

1905 - W. A. Smith, D.D.S.

1909 - Born in 1887, William D. McFadden began the practice of dentistry when he graduated from the University of Michigan in 1903. Served as a 1st Lieutenant in WWI. Following years of study on both the Seneca and Tonawanda Reservations, in 1929, he and his son were adopted into the Wolf Clan of the Seneca Indian Nation. He was given the name of TEG-WAN-DA meaning "arrowhead," Daniel's name was DA-WOH-ATA meaning "daylight." He was credited with unearthing an Indian Village on Oak Orchard Creek near Waterport. His extensive collection of arrowheads and other relics of the area were mounted in glass cases in his office, most of the time at 77 S. Main St., Middleport.

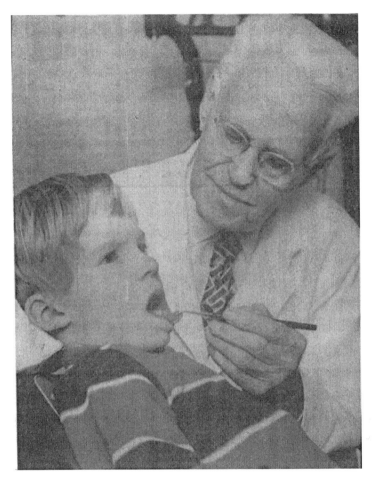

Born in 1887, Dr. William McFadden started his practice in Middleport in 1909. He continued to serve the community for 62 years until his retirement at the age of 93. He is shown here with Kent McKee, who was to be his last patient. Dr. McFadden died at the age of 100.
(Image from the Tri County News, Lockport 1971)

"Doc" had first treated his Indian friends on the Reservation; many of them came to his office for dental care. Chief Corbett Sundown said that during the depression Dr. McFadden would treat them at his office and didn't charge for the service.

On November 16, 1971 the Rotary Club honored "Doc" at a special meeting and the day was set aside in his honor. At the time he retired at the age of ninety-three he had always maintained a five-day-a-week schedule, saving Saturday mornings for children and others who could not get in during the week. When he retired he moved to Florida to be near his daughter, and died there at the age of 100.

1934 - John T. Lyon of Middleport graduated from the University of Buffalo; he was with the Eastman Dental Clinic, Rochester. Served as a dentist in the Army in WWII. Practiced in Middleport for more than fifty years.

1956 - Frank Pita opened an office at the corner of Main Street and Park Avenue; he was here for many years.

1968 - William Bellevia lived at Middleport, opened an office in Medina and then moved there.

1975 - Steve B. Gouw graduated from the University at Buffalo, and opened an office at 6 State Street. In 1979, he built an office on the site of the old theater at 26 Main Street. He received a Fellowship from the Academy of General Dentistry in 1985, and their Mastership Award in 1991. From 1990-1998, Dr. Todd Parlato was associated with his office.

He was received as a diplomat of the Board of the American Begg Association in 1996. In conjunction with Light Force Orthodontic he taught a group of Dutch dentists every three months completing their full two-year orthodontics course in 2000. He was selected to be included in the "Guide to American Top Dentists" by Consumers Research Council. He retired and moved to California to be near family.

2000 - Todd Parlato built his new office at 9754 Rochester Road.

2002 - Igor Kaplansky took over the practice of Steve Gouw at 26 Main Street. A native of Russia, he graduated from the University of Buffalo in 1998, receiving a Fellowship in the Academy of General Dentistry in 2003. He moved into his new office at 8038 Rochester Road, Gasport, in 2007.

A. Edmund Ferington received his dental degree from Loyola University in 1940, and served as an Army staff dental surgeon 1941-46 in the European Theater of Operations and N. African theaters. General George. H. Patton and Ambassador Henry Cabot Lodge were among his regular patients. He returned to Lockport and entered into private practice in 1947. Soon after, he married a Middleport resident and lived in Middleport for over forty years. He died in 1990.

Robert S. Mather of Stone Road received a degree in dental surgery in 1975, and opened an office in Florida where his family had located.

James E. Ferington received his dental degree from the University of Buffalo in 1979, and began practicing general dentistry with his father, A. E. Ferington.

----Jeffrey Bates received his degree from the University at Buffalo in 1995. He received training in laser surgery, and is practicing at Newfane Family Dentistry.

Drug Store

Prior to the Drug Store Licensing Act of 1904, anyone could call his business a "drug store," and many did. From 1870-1889 "Pharmacy on Niagara Frontier" listed several drug stores: Dr. Cassius W. Gould, Oliver R. Brown & Son (C. T. Brown), W. B. Garland, and L. S. Freeman. Peter Webber had a store on the right side of the Taylor Block next the canal from 1902-1910. Bensen & Fehrmann were listed in 1904, McDonald & Wallace were listed in 1916, and Wallace & Stringham were listed at 28 Main Street, 1933-38.

Augustus G. Taylor and Dr. F. L. Taylor lost their stores in fires on the same day in 1861, and the 1869 directory lists the Taylor brothers, Augustus G. and Charles B., at Main and State Streets, the beginning of 100 years of having a drug store at that location. In September 1879, it was reported that "Charles B. Taylor has moved into his new store, the 'knobbiest in town.'" This was after the January 1879 fire, and it has to be the present brick building at the corner of Main and State that has the canal scene mural on the side.

The Taylor stock was purchased in 1900. Owner Fred J. Haist hired Lewis S. Lampkins, who then purchased the store in 1916. Lampkins died in 1932 and his estate sold the store to Charles A. Moran of Lockport. In 1944 it became a Rexall store.

Drug stores were the logical outlets for distributing ice cream, as they used ice to cool the charged water for dispensing mineral water and flavored "soda water." Someone thought to add ice cream to the soda water and the ice cream soda was born! What a shame that there are a couple of generations of people who don't remember the long marble soda counter and the little round tables with the "ice cream" style chairs that the Lampkins store had.

Mr. Moran died in 1951 and the store was sold to Peterson Drug Co. of Oakfield, Donald Swift, manager. Middleport became the 16th branch of Peterson Drug, which was founded in 1926. In 1961 the business moved from 3 Vernon Street to the old Vary's Garage building where there was much more space, thus ending the drug store business on this corner. For many years the store had also been the Greyhound Bus terminal.

When the present Wilson Farm complex was built at 79-81 Rochester road, Hy-Tops Pharmacy opened in 1968. In 1978 Peterson Drug changed their location again and moved up there, selling to Bruce Moden and Steve Giroux in 1983. The firm is known as Middleport Family Health Center, and became a "Legend" pharmacy. The interior of the store was remodeled in about 2000, relocating the front checkout counter, and enlarging and relocating the pharmacy.

The southeast corner of State and Main has been a popular site for a drug store throughout the years. This photo shows Peterson's Drugs before it moved to the site of Mr. Vary's garage on Vernon Street. The old Rexall sign can be seen hanging in the Middleport Family Pharmacy on Route 31.
(Image from RTH)

Undertaking

The earliest reference that I have seen regarding the undertaking business was from an 1871 newspaper. "On the east side of Main Street near State, the cabinet shop of J. Compton, Jr. is filled with furniture of every description. In undertaking his business is extensive; his hearse is drawn by a $600 pair of black horses, handsome and richly caparisoned." In the same review, mention is made of "the new cabinet and undertaking establishment of Messrs Cheshire & Robertson on the north canal bank built in 1871. The building is two stories high, 22 feet by 72 feet, and the showroom contains an assortment of cabinet ware and coffins." And the building still survives.

From 1874, Mr. Compton was in business with E. Smith Freeman, Mr. Odell, and Ed Robinson, when they were located in the Eagle Block next to the canal until 1897, when his partner was George S. Bennett.

After the death of Compton, Bennett formed a partnership with Levi A. Whited, and in 1905, they were located in what became the police office and were advertising as "undertakers and embalmers." Whited assumed the business in 1906; in 1925 he was joined for a short time by E. I. Hill of Medina, and continued alone until his death in 1935.

Charles R. Richardson and Jerry Tracey were advertising in 1904 as "Richardson & Tracey Furniture and Funeral Directors," in the old Star Theater building at 26 Main Street, with C. J. Smith an associate. Tracey left the business for other endeavors, and in 1927, Herman A. Knuebel became a partner. In 1932, Richardson & Knuebel opened a funeral home in the large brick home at 38 State Street, which had been built in 1875 by Linus S. Freeman. Mr. Knuebel died suddenly in 1944 and Donald A. Heath entered the partnership.

On January 1, 1946 Warren B. Wallace purchased the interest of Mr. Richardson, and the firm became Wallace & Heath Funeral Home. It was incorporated in 1960. The porch was removed, and an addition was built all across the front, affording more space and ground level entrance. Wallace & Heath was joined by Dennis G. Bates in 1974, Mr. Bates becoming the sole owner and the name becoming Bates, Wallace & Heath, Inc.

The Keystone Group of Tampa, FL, a coalition of 100 preferred funeral homes acquired Bates, Wallace & Heath in 1999, and three homes in Niagara County and four in Orleans County. Keystone believes in allowing each firm to maintain their same management and services.

The furniture and undertaking business went together in the early days, as the furniture makers provided the coffins for burial, and the funeral might be held in a special back room at the furniture store, provided just for such services. Funerals were often conducted in the persons' home, where most often the embalming took place, and the

231

undertaker provided folding chairs for the funeral guests. A wreath would be placed on the front door.

From a local 1889 diary, after the death of a young girl, it was indicated that "we washed and dressed her in her prettiest dress, so that things would be ready when the undertaker came to fix the flowers."

"Undertakers" graduated to become "morticians" when embalming and body preparation became their responsibility. Before embalming was relied on completely as it is today, the casket was often an ice chest, looking like an oversized casket. The deceased would be placed on the bottom, which was usually metal lined with soldered seams. The top that was placed over it had an opening so that one could look in to view the face of the deceased. Another opening allowed the undertaker to put ice inside, to act as a coolant. With the advent of funeral homes the staff became known as "funeral directors."

Ridge Animal Hospital

Ridge Animal Hospital was started in 1965 by Dr. Thurston Dale at his home (at the time) on Ridge Road. Dr. Ronald F. Mayhew became his partner in 1967 and Dr. Kenneth Gumaer. The present hospital was built in 1973 at 3493 Stone Road. A large building for storage and the treatment of large farm animals was built in 1990. An open house was held in the fall of 1990 with Drs. Sandy Marky, Cynthia Lankenan, David G. Monti, and Paul A. Conner and all the staff conducting tours.

Ridge Animal Hospital ranks in an elite class, as fewer than 17% of small animal veterinary facilities in North America are accredited by the American Animal Hospital Association. Based on its high standards for hospitals and pet health care, Ridge Animal Hospital has been a member since 1977.

After the death of Dr. Mayhew in 1992, Dr. Dale was joined by Drs. Kenneth Gumaer and David Monti. In 1995 the Wright's Corners Animal Care Center was opened on Lake Avenue in Lockport to better serve the clients in that area and to ease the load at the Middleport office. Emergency calls were only handled at the Ridge Animal Hospital. The Avid Microchip was used as a means of identification.

Hotels

Around 1820 Levi Cole opened a hotel in a little log house that was the beginning of Middleport Village, on the southeast corner of Main and State Streets. Later, he changed locations and built a frame house on the opposite corner.

A sketch of the original Pierce Hotel, a wooden structure on the northeast corner of Main and State. Owner Horace Pierce made sure that a horse and wagon were always at the train station to pick up travelers staying at his hotel. (Image from Sanford & Co. <u>1878 Illustrated History of Niagara County</u>)

From the diary of Asa Fitch, with Professor Eaton and twenty students from Rensselaer Polytechnic Institute traveling the canal studying flora and fauna, he mentions staying "overnight at Middleport, May 17, 1826. The new hotel nearing completion will be the finest in the area."

In 1855, Horace Pierce became manager of the only hotel in Middleport. In 1871, the building was described as being 50 feet by 100 feet, with twenty sleeping rooms, several sitting rooms, billiard rooms and all modern appliances in vogue, and a dance hall 65 feet by 30 feet. It was referred to as being far above the ordinary class of country hotels. A. D. Rich became manager in 1876; the hotel burned in 1883.

After a fire destroyed the Pierce Hotel in 1883, new owner A.D. Rich rebuilt the hotel in brick.
(Image from RTH)

On the same site, at the northeast corner of Main and State Streets, the 118 feet by 47 feet Hotel Rich opened in 1885, built of brick. The hotel had an office, billiard room and bar, private double parlors, family rooms and large dining room on the main floor, eighteen large apartments on each of the second and third floors, which were "apparently beyond the needs of a town the size of Middleport." A. D. Rich was owner.

George Fenton owned the hotel until his retirement in 1944 and is shown here at its demolition in 1966. (Image from MVH)

George Fenton purchased the hotel in 1922, making extensive repairs and interior decorations, and it was then known as the Fenton Hotel. Fenton retired in 1944 and the hotel was lastly owned by Samuel Muscarrella, and after some years of disuse it was demolished in 1966. It was replaced by an auto service station, and later by the First Niagara Savings & Loan, now Cornerstone Credit Union.

The first hotel that we have seen mentioned on Vernon Street at "the Commons" was the Kimball House on the 1869 Town of Royalton census; Horace E. Kimball was the proprietor. A livery was attached.

On the 1875 insurance map this location was occupied by the Vernon House. A. D. Rich owned it when he first came here in about 1876. Aaron Martin was proprietor for a time, and also was when it first became the Grove House.

The Grove House was on the 1884 insurance map. "fronting on the public park." W. H. Dolson of Lockport leased the building, then making extensive improvements, and opening it as a hotel.

In 1887 a new law required that all hotels have a rope in each room above the first floor, in case of fire.

The Grove Hotel burned in 1896 "removing an old landmark." The Methodist Episcopal Church was built on the lot in 1899.

The Odell House was built north of the railroad tracks at South Vernon Street in 1893, and named in honor of owner James M. Odell; John D. Wilcox the proprietor. There was also an excellent barn for the accommodation of horses. In 1902 the contents of the house were to be sold at auction.

In 1906 it was the Chaswell Hotel, Willis Carrier, proprietor. W. F. Cramer became the owner in 1908 and changed the name to American Hotel. There were four other proprietors through the early 1950s when it became the Iron Horse, closing in about 1978. From 1991 there were several short-term proprietors, under several different names: Crystal Lounge, Sugar Mill, Town and Country Inn, Scott's Town and Country Inn, and the Middleport Inn. It closed in 2003.

Newspapers

For about 80 years Middleport had its own newspaper. In 1872 G. F. Marsh formerly of the Holley Standard, issued the first copy of the "Middleport Mail," a weekly paper located on Main Street.

In 1885 Julius A. Kuck, formerly of Kuckville, purchased the paper and did business under the name of "Middleport Herald." This was published on Thursdays in the Opera House Block. In 1908 Lewis A. Jones purchased the paper, and it came out semi-weekly on Tuesday and Friday.

The "Middleport Herald" was reorganized in 1922 when the paper was purchased by the Niagara Sprayer Company, and it became the "Niagara Herald." A lot was purchased at the corner of North Main and Mill Streets and their new building was erected the following year.

The first copy of the "Middleport Record" with Wm. J. Holahan, editor, and Roy L. Wheeler, Jr., publisher, both Middleport men, was issued December 1, 1949; it merged with the Herald-Tribune in 1951. On August 9, 1951 the paper was sold to Rochester attorney Francis M. Bradley.

*Home of the Middleport Record, run by Wm. Holahan
and Roy Wheeler on State Street.
(Image from collection of Wm. Holahan)*

The Hammond Gazette

The "Hammond Gazette," while not a true newspaper to the publishing world, was a link from home to many a serviceman.

Starting as a letter to two Middleport youths during WWII, it grew to a hectographed, legal-sized edition containing a minimum of six pages. It was eagerly read by Middleport troops stationed in the four corners of the globe, and very often by their friends no matter where they were from. The letter was sent free to all area service people, the only price was a correct address and a smile. The initial issue was sent October 18, 1943 and continued for almost two years, only missing two issues.

The final copy of the paper was published the day after V-J Day. At that time 230 copies containing local news, jokes, letters from addresses of servicemen, and articles by local residents were mailed each week. The paper was financed by donations from parents, relatives and friends of the addressees as well as from some of the business organizations in the village.

Ray Hammond edited the paper from his home in his spare time. He said that the project would not have been possible without "the group" of a dozen teenage reporters and two adults, and his wife, Gladys, operated the secondhand mimeograph machine. Before the paper was suspended, two of the staffers were lost to the staff of Uncle Sam.

1944 staff of the Hammond Gazette. Front row: Tim Tracey, Willard Pomeroy and Ray Hammond, Back row: Peggy Thaxter, Mary Tracey, Claire Ann Whittaker, Mary Thaxter and Jean Martin.
(Image from the Wm. Holahan Collection and Claire Whittaker Allen)

In February 1946 when the majority of those who had received the Gazette were again civilians, never again to be the "boys" who went to war, Ray was the guest of honor at a banquet held by Clute-Phillips American Legion Post #938.)

In 1951 Mr. Hammond completed twenty years of service with the New York Central Railroad as a crossing watchman. When he started on the job he worked twelve hours a day, seven days a week!

Middleport Gremlin Dodger

In 1943 the War Bond Campaign for Niagara County had doubled the goal of 2.5 million dollars, and on May 16th many residents, dignitaries and war effort organizations met at the Buffalo Airport to christen eighteen P-40 War Hawk fighters and three C-46 Commando transport planes.

Middleport had financed a $45,000 Curtiss-Wright P-40 War Hawk through war bond purchases; the Middleport Rotary Club held a "name plane" contest at the high school because of excellent school participation. Names were submitted by all the classes, and the name selected was "Middleport Gremlin Dodger." Senior Kevin Bunnell was named to christen the plane at the ceremony.

Ten minutes after the ceremony, the "Gremlin Dodger" crashed at the north end of the airport. Witnesses said that as it pulled out of a double loop and a sharp turn, it was about to hit the ground when it pulled out and rose, striking the wires above the New York Central Railroad tracks nearby. The plane burst into flames, nosedived to earth and was smashed to bits; the pilot was killed. Guests at the ceremony did not see the accident.

The thirty-five-year-old test pilot, Hugh Van Alstyne of Kinderhook, NY, had been a pilot for nine years; he had logged more than 5000 air hours. He worked for the Buffalo

Aeronautical Corporation and Pennsylvania Central Airlines with the rank of captain.

The Middleport Gremlin Dodger, shortly before taking off and crashing at the Buffalo Airport, killing the pilot. Shown in photo are (left to right): Leo J. Coleman, Warren Snell and Kevin P. Bunnell. (Image from Media Journal Register)

Co-chairmen of the Middleport Bonds Committee Leo J. Coleman and Warren Snell were heartbroken over the death of pilot Van Alstyne. "Though we can do nothing to replace him, we are determined to replace the plane."

The Curtiss-Wright Corporation of Buffalo was the major producer of aircraft during WWII, and made 14,000 War Hawks.

Ku Klux Klan

A branch of the Ku Klux Klan was instituted in Middleport with the burning of a fiery cross, on May 10, 1924.

From 1922 until 1925, Western New York was a hotbed of Klan activities; Binghamton was the State headquarters from 1923-1924. The Klan of this era was more widespread nationally than the original Klan that flourished in the Reconstruction South.

On Saturday, June 6, 1925, a Klan meeting was held on the Gursslin farm on the north side of the canal, east of the village, attended by about 1500-2000 Klansmen and "invited spectators and others." At a similarly large meeting at Albion, none of the paraders were from the central and western Orleans County. As the autos passed through the village, the business district was crowded and the sidewalks lined with people trying to get a glimpse of the white-robed and hooded occupants.

They had a band, two refreshment stands, and a class of men and a class of women were initiated into the Order. Two fiery crosses were burned. During the meeting the street had been strewn with large tacks for two blocks, and on the way to the high bridge and for a mile down the road slow leaks caused the tires to go down. During a good part of Sunday, men and children picked tacks from the dust and gravel.

The second wave of Klan activity swept the United States, driven in a large part by fear of immigrants. Explaining why they didn't welcome Catholics, Jews or Negroes as members, they wanted only Caucasians who had their allegiances confined within the boundaries of the United States They were organized to maintain American principles, opposed to lawlessness and lack of Americanism. They were opposed to aliens coming into the United States, becoming wealthy and not thinking enough of America to become citizens or to obey its laws.

In 1925, two Middleport men were held by police in Niagara Falls after being charged with sending letters on behalf of the KKK.

Inventors

The Director of the United States Patent Office recommended in 1898 that the office be abolished, because everything that was ever going to be invented had already been invented and patented. That was how many years ago?!!

Middleport had a long list of inventors, and many apologies to those of whom we have no record. Several patents were assigned to their companies by the employees.

Adelbert Acer was granted a patent for a fruit basket fastener in 1930.

Carl Allgrun was a quiet man with a little machine shop behind his house. He devised a method of boring gun barrels and coastal defense guns in one operation. A grateful nation used his invention in WWI, but the government didn't "reward" him until he brought a suit for a million dollars.

Linus Burghardt in about 1900 invented a bicycle tire inflator. He also patented a combination bicycle rack and automatic bicycle pump: drop a penny in the slot and the machine pumped up the tire.

Ernest B. Freeman produced a gas powered pump to spray fruit orchards that won a Gold Medal Award at the St.

Louis Exposition in 1904. Its production was the foundation of Niagara Sprayer Co., now known as FMC.

Edward Knapp invented the Knapp Giant Bean Picker in 1892. This was used to clean and sort beans for market that was manufactured here until the early 1900s when the patent was sold.

Elgie J. Lewis was a volunteer firefighter, he rigged up a line between the boiler in the village hall and the boiler on the 1893 fire engine; a coupling would separate the two and the pumper was ready to go to a fire, already charged with steam. A foreman at the Ontario Preserving Co. he devised a machine that would pare the pineapples that they were importing from Hawaii, and he later added slicing and coring capabilities.

In 1912, Lewis engineered the cannery's first string bean cutter that was used by Campbell Soup Co. for years, also used for celery, okra, carrots and rhubarb.

He also invented the Lewis Power Can Tester to test the Ontario Preserving Company metal cans for leaks. It was also used by the Edison Battery Co. to test metal containers for their new electric automobile being produced at the time.

Arthur D. McDonald was working at Cadillac Motor Division, GMC, where he was assigned to design and develop an automatic transmission for busses. This same basic transmission was used on tanks during WWII.

In the 1950s he licensed a pump design which he developed into the Sigma motor pump, allowing a radical new procedure in heart surgery, making him a pioneer in the field of biomedical engineering. During his career as an engineer, he received well over 100 patents for machine products used in the diverse fields of medicine, chemistry, food processing and printing.

Judith Schwan was educated in chemical engineering. She joined Eastman Kodak Co. in 1950 as a research scientist. Moving through the ranks of management, she retired as director of their Photographic Research Laboratories. Along the way she acquired twenty-one patents, and in 1979 she received the top award from the Motion Picture and Television Engineers for her work in color films. In 1982, she was elected to the National Academy of Engineering.

George Smith patented and manufactured barrel tools, hoop bending machines, and invented a machine that would finish both ends of a barrel at the same time.

David Snell invented an extension ladder for general use but it was very good for firemen as advertised in the 1896 New York State Firemen's Association official souvenir program.

Elmer Vary went to work at the canning factory as a youngster, as his father, Jay S. Vary, was superintendent, processor and chemist, and one of the founders of the Ontario Preserving Co. in 1883. His father never bothered to patent the wire snap that he devised to hold the covers onto glass canning jars that Mason, Ball, Atlas and others used for years.

Newspaper ad for Mr. Vary's invention of the cherry pitter, not only for home use but also for the canning factory where it helped speed up the preserving of fresh cherries for the market.
(Image from MVH)

Elmer produced thirty-five inventions relating to the canning industry, only seven of which he bothered to patent. Among them were two cherry pitting machines. At the age of sixteen he made his first model for industrial use that pitted 300 cherries per minute. He also patented a pineapple eyer, a peach slicer, a filter for steam pipes and an automatic can marker, for until then there was no way to tell who had canned the product or what was in the can.

Mark D. Williams, a local veterinary surgeon, and Ernest Brown invented a potato cutter and planter in 1890. The machine would cut and plant the potatoes as fast as the horses could walk, with no skips.

E. L. Downey, M.D., invented and patented a liquid insecticide to be used on fruit trees, founding the Downicide Chemical Co.

On Dec. 6, 1909, two Middleport men filed a patent on a potato paring machine.

On Oct. 7, 1935 a device used to turn fruit baskets for packing was patented at Middleport.

B-Kwik Super Market, Wilson Farms

On June 19, 1969, Mayor Elton E. Birch officiated at the ribbon cutting for the grand opening of the new B-Kwik Super Market, located at 79 Rochester Road. It was owned by Philip Bokan of Cambria, and managed by Robert Remington. Mr. Bokan became manager in 1972.

Many years ago the grocery became a Wilson Farms store. A grand re-opening was held in mid-2008 in celebration of recent remodeling. The store now offers a full-service deli, an expanded produce selection and an overall increase in product varieties; a made-to-order Sub Shoppe and hand-scooped Perry ice cream flavors, and Red Box video rentals. It is now a real, albeit small, "super market"!

The Green Kettle, Stop #31, Darrell's Place

Ernest Swarthout of Middleport purchased land on the northeast corner of Kelly Avenue and Route 31 with the intention of building a small motel primarily for truck drivers. In about 1950, Clare Gilbert moved a small building to the lot and sold cemetery stones.

The original Green Kettle, now the location of Darrell's Place on the corner of Route 31 and Kelly Avenue. (Image from RTH)

Swarthout and Floyd Halstead opened a small restaurant on the site in 1954, with Marge Green as the cook. On the death of Swarthout, the partnership was dissolved, and the restaurant was purchased by Mrs. Green and was known as the "Green Kettle" until she closed in 1979. For a time it was known as "Barb's Place."

The restaurant was purchased by Martin C. Murphy of Lockport in 1982, and "Stop #31" expanded on the west side to afford a private dining room for fifty, with a total seating capacity of ninety-six. After ten years Murphy opened "Murph's Restaurant" at Town Square, Lockport, and Darrell Gillbert of Middleport became manager at "Stop #31." Darrell has been the owner of "Darrell's Place" since 1996.

The Basket Factory

An article in the June 1886 Niagara Herald reported that logs were being received at the (Sylvester J.) Evans & (Henry) McClean Basket Factory. The plant turned out about 2000 baskets a day.

The original structure of the Royalton Basket Factory, now the site of the empty restaurant on the Erie Canal. (Image from RTH)

James Hulihan and his brother-in-law, Thomas Conley, formed a partnership and opened the Royalton Basket Company on the site of the present Basket Factory Restaurant in 1893 to meet the demand for bushel baskets for fruit from local orchards shipped on the canal. All sizes of baskets from bushel baskets to berry baskets and crates were made there.

Logs were tied together to form a raft and floated down the canal, or purchased from area farmers, and were held in the log pond, the present marina. The logs were lifted from the pond with a crane, taken into the factory on a dolly, cut into six-foot lengths and steamed in vats on the lower level. When the material was needed, long narrow strips were peeled by a lathe. The strips were then put in a wheelbarrow and taken to the top floor in the elevator. There the baskets were assembled, stapled and the handles attached. The building to the east of the restaurant was a storage building; a steam-heated conveyor connected it to the top floor of the factory. The baskets dried as they traveled to the warehouse.

Delivery wagon bringing baskets to local farmers throughout the area.
(Image from RTH)

Baskets were delivered to area farmers by horse and wagon, and it was said that the horses knew the way back to the factory, so the driver could nap on the return trip. From about 1920 until closing in 1934, the Royalton Basket Company was owned by James H. and Timothy J. O'Shaughnessy.

Two brothers, James F. Harmon, a Buffalo high school principal, and John J., a Buffalo firefighter, purchased the old building in 1968, as the marina was an ideal place to park a houseboat that they had just built. They spent four years restoring the old building, and then opened it as a restaurant. In 1978 it was purchased by Sharon Shaefer, and was known as "Shaefer's Basket Factory Restaurant," which she operated very successfully until 1997. The "loft" held parties for up to sixty people beginning in 1989.

After two short-term sales and a brief closure, it was opened again in the summer of 2001 by sisters Julie Riegel and Dawn Thompson, offering lunch and dinner six days a week and Sunday brunch, frequent music by local performers and outdoor dining on the patio, in season. Roughly hewn barn beams and hundreds of hanging baskets, and a canal-side view from lace-adorned windows in a warm and relaxed setting are part of the charm of the Basket Factory.

Bert Resseugie & Son, W. H. Rhinehart, Inc.

Bert Resseugie opened a flour and feed store under the Braddock meat market on State Street in 1908; Bert Resseugie & Son was established in 1912.

Their first mill was in back of the Wheeler Coal Yard in 1931, between Maple Avenue and the railroad, with a capacity of forty barrels in twenty-four hours. In 1937, they purchased the Albert Harrington building shown on the 1905 insurance map, a fruit warehouse just west of Jackson's bean house. A floor space of 14,400 square foot tripled the size of their old building, and was equipped with bag elevators and feed chutes.

They sold "Even Better" self-rising health flour, "Reliable" self-rising buckwheat flour, and "Pure Pancake" flour, "Three Roses" pastry flour, and "Home Pride" all purpose flour.

The Resseugie name was one of the oldest in New York State milling, dating back to about 1875, with Irving Resseugie of North Ridgeway. Mr. Arthur Resseugie had been in the feed and milling business in this area for thirty years beginning in 1920. In 1949, razing began on the local landmark that had been their location in 1931.

Wilbur H. Rhinehart purchased the complex at 18 Orchard Street in 1973, handling grain, feed and fertilizer. The former Harrington building burned in 1979.

Gradually they began carrying quite a line of work clothes: boots, Carolina and Wolverine shoes, Outback and Wrangler Western wear, Dickie and Bibs, and women's Carhartt; plus bird seed, cat and dog food, etc. A warehouse was built in the mid-1990s, and a new office building in 2005 made the third in their new complex at 4133 Carmen Road.

Barden And Robeson Corporation

The complex that is now Barden Homes has been the home of four different types of woodworking businesses since 1890. The first was Middleport Manufacturing Company which produced interior house furnishings until 1896. Locally it was referred to as the "Sash and Blind."

Royalton Door operated from 1896-1898.

Niagara Wood Works continued to manufacture indoor house trim, 1909-1914. A former employee said that the pay was 10¢ per hour for a ten-hour-day, six days a week.

Niagara Wood Works, now the location of Barden Homes
on Kelly Ave by the railroad tracks.
(Image from MVH)

Niagara Furniture Company, from 1919 to the mid-1930s, made parlor furniture. In 1917 they were makers of high-grade walnut and mahogany dining room furniture. Theodore Dosch, vice-president; Edward F. Lahey, secretary and manager; George Thompson, treasurer.

Barden and Robeson purchased the woodworking plant in the early 1940s, mainly making ammunition boxes and crates during WWII.

The Barden name has been identified with affordable quality construction since 1909. The family owned and operated business started with bushel baskets and wagon wheels, expanding to baby furniture in 1929, becoming a national supplier to Sears and Montgomery Ward.

The first Barden home was constructed in 1947, which pioneered the panelized manufacturing process at Middleport, and is also known for doing commercial buildings and churches. Barden Homes has developed a family-owned business into a nationally recognized leader in the home industry, providing quality, energy efficient homes to thousands of satisfied customers.

A new 35,000 square foot, multi-million dollar production facility was opened in 2004. It was announced in 2006 that a 14,000 square foot expansion with a new, model high-tech office complex and building operations center would be built on Route 31 to accommodate the sales growth in Western New York, Ohio and Canada.

On November 8, 2006, a million dollar fire of electrical origin completely destroyed the wall department building, and damaged a building nearby. Until the building is back up and running again, production was temporarily shifted to the company's facility near Syracuse. The Middleport plant is now able to handle the current demand.

Four generations of Bardens are active in the company, employing 250-285 people at the Middleport site.

Niagara Sprayer Co., Niagara Sprayer & Chemical Co., Inc., Food Machinery Corporation - Niagara Chemical Division, FMC Corporation - Agricultural Chemical Group

Middleport native Ernest B. Freeman recognized the need of the Niagara Frontier fruit producing area for a spraying machine to control orchard pests and diseases. In 1904 he was granted a patent for a gas spraying machine to blanket the orchards with the limited number of sprays then existing, such as Paris Green or Bordeaux. One of the first machines was taken to the Louisiana Purchase Exposition that year, where it was awarded a gold medal and blue ribbon.

As a result, Mr. Freeman interested a group of financers in promoting the manufacture and sale of his invention. This was the beginning of the Niagara Sprayer Co., Inc. in 1904. Work was done on the Freeman farm just south of the village, and the business office was at the L. S. Freeman Bank Building. The company moved briefly to Perry Street, Buffalo, and then to Middleport to the Opera House Block.

Early financers of Mr. Freeman's invention and the start up of the Niagara Sprayer. From left to right: Edgar Knapp, inventor of his own bean picker, State Senator George Thompson who served as secretary, Charles Shafer, treasurer and Theodore Dosch, first plant manager. (Image from collection of Wm. Holahan)

In 1907, the operation was taken over by National Aniline Chemical Works of Buffalo. They built a lime and sulfur solution plant at Middleport, and abandoned the gas sprayer for a gasoline-powered pressure pump. The cost of shipping a water solution largely limited the sale to the Western New York fruit belt (which at the time was the nation's leading area for production of quality fruit). A National Aniline chemist invented a method for a soluble sulfur compound that could be shipped in dry form. A plant for its production was built at Middleport, and the company's expansion program began. Additional sprays and dusts supplied a full line of pesticides and application equipment to the agricultural market.

In 1914 Ernest Hart, an entomologist, graduated from Michigan State College and joined the company, beginning its first technical department, eventually becoming head of FMC.

The sting of the recessions after WWI hit the fruit and chemical industries hard, and in the 1920s the organizers branched out into other ventures: The Niagara Warehouse Co., Niagara Herald Co., Niagara Housing Development Co., Niagara Furniture Co., Royalton Basket Co. and Rochester Rex Co.

Opening of the machine shop and dusting machine assembly plant of Niagara Sprayer on December 2, 1921. (Image from MVH)

On December 2, 1921, a community banquet opened the machine shop and dusting machine assembly plant of the

Niagara Sprayer Co. In February 1923, a $100,000 arsenic acid plant was completed, with a capacity of seventeen tons per day. As a result of the expanded production line, in 1927 the company became known as the Niagara Sprayer & Chemical Co. They had branch plants in Jacksonville, Florida; San Francisco, California; and Burlington, Ontario, Canada. The complete reorganization in 1928 put the company on a strong footing; Alfred Schoellkopf became president and held the post until he died. The company was becoming a dominant factor in the industry and his controlling interest was acquired by Food Machinery Corporation of San Jose, California.

Niagara Sprayer facility in 1923, looking east along railroad track with the present-day deserted Norco building on the left side.
(Image from RHCL)

The company grew and the list of key people living locally would read like a Middleport Village Directory and a good cross-section of Medina. Long after it became FMC, veteran workers still made reference to "working at the Sprayer."

Research and development was centered in the multi-million dollar facility at Middleport, erected in 1961 and 1963. As part of the research activities their three large farms were located at Gasport, New York; Marion, Arkansas; and Davis, California.

Until 1975, the main headquarters for ag-chem crop protection research was at Middleport, the international nerve center of that part of the FMC business. Then it was decided to move the division headquarters to Philadelphia. With that move came the decision not to expand research at Middleport. Research was consolidated at Princeton, New Jersey, and in 1982 the Middleport research facility was closed.

The James R. Jones FMC Agricultural Chemical Plant in Uberaba, Brazil, was the first FMC construction anywhere to be named in honor of an individual. As manager of international manufacturing, the long-time FMC executive and Middleport resident headed the construction in 1979 for the manufacture of the highly successful Furadan compound.

Furadan was discovered and developed at the Middleport Research Facility, and locally Middleport is called "the Furadan center of the world." An insecticide-nematicide, it is used in eighty countries on fifty crops for the control of more than 300 insect pests.

On November 15, 1984, a thirty to fifty gallon spill of the chemical methyl isocyanate (MIC) at the plant brought a great deal of concern and public criticism from the community as some of the MIC vaporized and went into the open vents of the nearby Royalton-Hartland Elementary school. The ventilation system at the Junior-Senior High School had been shut down and prevented any fumes from getting in. Emergency plans were in place and had been used, and they worked. School Superintendent Dr. William Bassett said that the person most responsible for the plans was FMC Safety Officer Lou Rotella. Clean up work went on for weeks and scores of other actions and meetings followed, both in an attempt to find causes of possible dangers, and to take corrective and preventative actions. Also in the aftermath were federal and state inquiries as well as county and local inquiries, and there were also some adjustments within the FMC plant. Soon after the accident here, forty tons of the chemical spilled in Bhopal, India, killing 2500 people on December 3rd, intensifying the local concern.

The company proved to be responsive to the concerns voiced by the citizen groups and the United States Environmental Protection Agency, the New York State Department of Environmental Conservation and the New York State Department of Health. Frequent Environmental Protection Agency and Department of Environmental Conservation public involvement sessions have been held, and soil cleanup projects have been ongoing for some years.

One of the largest Interim Corrective Measures performed was removal of contaminated soil from the Royalton-Hartland School football and athletic field area, and the bus parking lot. During excavation and field restoration the field could not be used. Desiring to be a good neighbor and in cooperation with the school and their schedules they wanted to provide the community with benefits that would outweigh the inconveniences caused by the project.

An interim football field was constructed on the Gasport Elementary sports field. A new baseball field, and lights to illuminate both the baseball and football fields, were constructed at the Gasport School to be ready for the fall 1999 season. The improvements at Middleport were the new football field, a new all-weather track, a new press box, concession stand, storage area, restrooms and new lights, ready for the fall of 2000. An architectural firm contacted for the work designed the Buffalo Bills practice field and other athletic facilities in Western New York.

In cooperation with the Federal and State Agencies, in 2003 soils were replaced at ten residences adjacent to the plant on Vernon Street, two properties on South Vernon Street, and two properties on Main Street that were in the historic water drainage pathway from the plant. Residents had to leave their homes for two weeks while the work was being done. Excavation was from 6 inches to 54 inches deep, based on previous soil sampling.

The Community Advisory Panel (CAP) was formed in 1998 with eighteen residents of the Gasport-Middleport area meeting about once a month. They publish the "Viewpoints" newsletter to provide residents with information regarding community issues, FMC plant activities and environmental concerns. "FMC Community

Connection" is published several times a year. The public is periodically invited to an Open House and plant tour.

FMC has established a Middleport community website, www.teapothollow.com; the company offers a Property Price Protection program; information about the sites and results of any of the studies and documents are available for inspection locally at the Middleport Free Library or online.

For several years FMC has been presenting $100 scholarships and personalized plaques each year to the Royalton-Hartland students excelling in biology, mathematics and chemistry.

Middleport Task Force

In 1987 the Mayor's Task Force received the Community Awareness & Response Program Level II recognition award from the Chemical Manufacturer's Association.

The task force was created in the fall of 1984 by Mayor Harold Mufford just a few weeks before the expiration of his term of office to coordinate local emergency planning and preparedness activities in the village following the chemical spill at FMC.

Monthly meetings have taken place involving the mayor's office, fire and police departments, State police, Niagara County Sheriff's Department, FMC Corporation, Royalton-Hartland Central Schools, Tri-Town Ambulance Service, Eastern Niagara American Red Cross, the County Emergency Management Office and Radio Amateur Civil Emergency Service.

There are about 1100 task force groups in the country, and the Middleport group is one of only thirty to win the Level II award that requires local planning committees to complete several requirements.

E & M Enterprises

E & M Enterprises was formed in 1937 by Arthur D. McDonald of Middleport, a graduate of General Motors Institute, and Robert Ebbert of Michigan, and later joined by his brother Frederick, operating in a small way at his father's garage at 69 Main Street. Soon the tool and die business moved to the stone VanBrocklin building at 3 Vernon Street. The following year they began doing work for Curtiss-Wright, who was building planes for France. The years 1939-1945 brought expansion, with work for several other companies involved in work for the war effort.

The plant operated twenty-four-hours-a-day, six days a week, producing parts for Harrison Radiator, GMC; Buffalo Arms, Sterling Engine, Chrysler, etc. Employment averaged twenty-six people, and about that time many young trainees were lost to the draft; several older people were hired, including three women. The war was winding down, and until 1962, they were able to contract for civilian purposes, expanding into machinery design, development and manufacture. The customer list still included Harrison Radiator, adding Kodak, DuPont, Moore Business Forms, Lapp Insulator and several smaller companies. Employment grew from war-time twenty-six to nearly 100, with a long-time average of sixty-five. Moore Business Forms became the largest customer as E & M built prototype equipment in connection with their research and subsequent production modules.

During this time five high school graduates were sponsored at the University of Cincinnati in a co-op program, and all of them graduated after serving in the armed forces. Two of them established their own businesses while the others returned to E & M as full-time employees.

In 1951, a new plant was built on the west side of Kelly Avenue to accommodate expansion and to improve facilities. Borden Inc. purchased E & M in 1962, with Mr. McDonald as consultant and development engineer, making process and equipment improvements at several plants, especially in the cheese plants. He remained as consultant for Borden until 1973, when he moved to North Carolina. In 1987, E & M Division was sold to Alcoa Aluminum; in 1991, it was purchased by Marsh Engineering of Port Colbourne, Ontario, making it the cornerstone of their United States operations. The plant was closed in 2003.

Sigma Motor

Soon after the war, Van Hungerford was employed at E & M, where he became sales engineer. Through his contacts they obtained a finger pump that could be adapted to any number of uses, as the substance being used didn't touch the pump. E & M obtained the license, redesigned the pump and set up a corner of the shop to produce the Sigma Motor Pump. Van led in promoting sales and Sigma Motor became a division of E & M in 1951 with Van Hungerford as president. They began producing the Sigma Motor heart pump in 1953.

Van and Arthur McDonald witnessed the fourth open heart operation performed at the University of Minnesota hospital by Drs. Lillie and Varco. This led to interest by other surgeons for other pumps made to special specifications. As demand increased Sigma Motor was sold to Van in 1954. Within fifteen years about 3000 heart pumps were sold. In the 1960s the "heart game" became very competitive, and Van conferred at Cleveland Clinic on the design of a kidney dialysis machine. About 7000 were in use by the late 1980s.

From Sigma Motor came three other companies: Sigma Inc began in Middleport in 1982 by Van's son Roger; American Sigma also began in 1982 by son William. A third, Cormed Inc., was begun by Gerald Hilger who had worked for Van for 25 years. Variations of pumps are the core of their products.

Sigma Motor building on the corner of Mill and Main Street. (Image from MVH)

Devam, Inc.

Devam Inc. was started by A. D. McDonald in 1964 in the Plastimold building, Telegraph Road, doing mechanical design and development work, with the bulk of the work for Borden and Devam. A soft cheese plant was changed from a small-batch process to a many times greater mechanized batch. Designed, mechanized, built and tested at Devam, the improvement paid off for Borden in 3 years. Several food processes were mechanized for other Borden plants. A machine was designed, tested, and built for making coffee filters.

Some large prototype machines for Moore Business Forms included special printing presses and other equipment for new business form products. In 1971, Devam was sold to Moore Business Forms for a prototype facility for their research division, later merging into a new facility on Grand Island.

Huntingdon Analytical Services Inc.

Opening in October 1985, dedication of the British-owned company the Huntingdon Analytical Services facility was celebrated with a ribbon-cutting and a two gun salute by the King's Regiment from Old Fort Niagara. Huntingdon Analytical Services is a subsidiary of Huntingdon International Holdings PLC, one of the world's largest firms specializing in chemical analysis.

After two years of contacts with development agencies, there were several reasons for locating in western New York. The proximity of major universities offered a strong technical labor force. The first staff of nineteen employees all came from the Buffalo-Rochester area. Middleport is accessible to both Buffalo and Rochester airports and to New York City. The company is located in the renovated 66,000 square foot FMC research facility on Route 31 that was designed as a chemical laboratory.

Huntingdon was founded in 1951 as a nutritional research company in England. Richard J. Ronan was general manager of the Middleport complex. Huntingdon Analytical Services is a division of Empire Soils Investigations, Inc. of Hamburg, New York. Four laboratories were located at the local facility: The Federal Insecticide, Fungicide and Rodenticide Acts lab. The largest is the environmental laboratory, testing on soil, water, and air samples. There was an asbestos lab, doing three main tests. The geo-technical lab tests the results of drilling, and different types of materials that make up the soil. There were about ninety people employed at Middleport.

In July 1994, the United States subsidiary was put up for strategic review, a move that could lead to its sale.

Monroe Electronics

Monroe Electronics was founded in Rochester in 1953. It was a pioneer in the development of instruments for the accurate measurement of static electrical charges without the hazard of physical contact. Robert E. Vosteen devised and patented electro static equipment that satisfied problems that both Kodak and Haloid, now Xerox, had been having. The small business was mainly in the realm of measurement and control.

Operations were moved to Middleport in 1958 to the old E & M Enterprises building on Vernon Street. In 1972, they moved to Lyndonville when larger facilities were needed, to the former DuPont plant on Housel Avenue.

They have about twenty products that are shipped all over the United States and used by several major corporations including Kodak, DuPont and 3-M. Internationally, about 15% of their shipments go to Japan and Europe.

The cable program switching and timing equipment is used by cable companies for distributing transmission from their headquarters to the individual cable customers. When the television viewers experience technical difficulties and are instructed to "do not adjust your set," the Monroe video sensor aids in returning the program intact.

The "encoder sensor" senses the loss of a scramble signal, assuring that an adult or pay-per-view channel stays off the air as directed. The company also manufactures remote control and tone signaling products for use in security monitoring fields.

While serving as a director of the Electrostatic Society of America in 1982, Mr. Vosteen was invited to deliver a paper at the International Conference on Charged Particles at Southampton, England, on the management of electrostatic problems.

Plastimold

Plastimold built a new $100,000 plant at 80 Telegraph Road in 1956 and operations started even before the plant was completed, with Carl Burton as assistant manager. Sydney Porter, vice-president, was the inventor of a number of processes in the manufacture of vinyl footwear, and was responsible for manufacturing operations and research and development. Edward H. Goddard, a long time associate of Mr. Porter was plant engineer and operating superintendent.

In 1957 Plastimold became the subsidiary of Tyer Rubber Company of Andover, Mass., "making footwear for the families of America." Philip McLean was resident manager. Plastimold Inc. was sold to Converso Rubber of Malden, Massachusetts, and in 1961 the local plant was closed.

By turns the plant has been occupied by Devam, Inc; Loud-Wendel, Inc; Devpro Machine, Inc; CMSB Magnetics. Recently the space has been shared by Birch Machine & Tool, Hydro Fabrication, Performance Manufacturing and Xpertek Electronics.

Loud-Wendel, Inc.

Loud-Wendel was incorporated in 1946 by Glen F. Loud of Gasport, and H. Schoelles Wendel of Middleport, both executives at Harrison Radiator Division, General Motors Corporation (GMC). The manufacturer of circular wood-cutting saws was located at 66 Main Street.

In 1951, controlling interest of the plant with 100 employees was purchased by Skillsaw, Inc. of Chicago. A 6000 square foot expansion was undertaken in 1958; in 1967 they moved 80 Telegraph Road, Route 31. In 1979 production was moved to Skokee, Illinois, and the Middleport plant was closed.

F. A. Whittaker Co., Inc.

Founded in 1889, the store progressed into the hands of the third generation of management. Through its early years it was in turn: a confectionary store, a pool hall, a cigar store, a bakery, and a bicycle shop. They were the Village's first Ford dealer, when one of the models had a gas tank mounted on the back of the car. The store had the first gas pump in 1909 - before that gas was sold by the barrel.

At the end of WWII "Buzz," or Francis A., purchased the William Whittaker Company from his father, and hired his father to assist in its management.

Under the name of F. A. Whittaker Co., Inc., the firm was chiefly involved with the distribution of Socony-Mobil petroleum products, with a bulk plant on Francis Street, and served by the New York Central Railroad. They also owned a service station on the southwest corner of State and Vernon Streets. It received petroleum in various forms from the bulk plant, via the company's four 1500-gallon tank trucks.

The store housed a variety of electrical appliances, plumbing materials, sporting goods, furnaces and boilers, boats and outboard motors, and everything in the tobacco line.

The firm was an authorized Westinghouse dealer, and handled the Richmond plumbing line, Oneida Royal furnaces, Peter ammunition, West Bend marine equipment and Starcraft boats. The Main Street establishment served as the home base for a truck and crew that provided plumbing and heating installation and service.

Gould's Greenhouse

John Henry Gould, or "J.H." as he was called, was a gardener for a well-to-do English family, arriving here in 1875. He grew his first crop of vegetables in Middleport. He built a small greenhouse to start seedlings, growing vegetables and flowers that he sold on alternate days in Medina and Batavia from his high-wheeled Democrat wagon.

Gould's Flowers, located at the present site of Dr. Stahl's medical offices, has a shop still offering flowers in the city of Lockport. The greenhouses fell out of use in 1967 and were eventually demolished.
(Image from RTH)

When cheaper vegetables were shipped by railroad, "J.H." switched entirely to flowers. He began with calla lilies and violets, the favorites of the Victorian era ladies, shipping them to the Buffalo market by trolley. He branched out, growing other types of flowers and began selling complete arrangements from the greenhouse on N. Hartland Street. Two children, Charles and Lola, joined the family business; retail shops were added in Albion and Medina, and in Lockport in the 1930s.

John Gould had only been here for fifteen years when he was the leader of the Middleport Cornet Band. In the early 1930s the Greenhouse Band held Saturday night concerts on Main Street.

During WWII, German POWs housed at Fort Niagara were sent out to work in the area, including at Gould's Flowers. They were often unhappy, not only missing their homes but simple things like lunches of homemade bread and butter and milk. Charles' wife began baking bread, Lola churned butter, and with fresh milk the POWs would argue to see who would go to Gould's. Werner Sachs was only seventeen years old, and Lola took him under her motherly wing; he kept in touch with her after the war. He made a name for himself in Germany as an artist, and sent twenty-one sketches to the Niagara County Historical Society in her memory.

Establishing his business in 1878 as a market gardener, by 1908 "J. H." had the largest and most up-to-date plant between Rochester and Buffalo. There were twelve greenhouses on nine acres of land, one house occupying more than an acre of ground and covered by 25,000 square foot of glass. All planting and potting was done in a central location; J.H. built things to last, and made cement potting benches instead of the usual redwood. Competition couldn't get second-year growth as he could - the secret was in changing the soil each year. They had their own water supply from a local creek.

A 350-horsepower boiler used 1000 tons of coal each winter to heat the greenhouses. In the beginning, the coal cost 60¢ a ton. A ten-ton ice machine refrigerated the cut flowers.

They raised everything that they sold: roses, carnations, orchids, gardenias, and just about anything else you could name. They became affiliated with FTD in 1932, and they would find the telegraph orders under the office door when arriving at work. Charles and Edith Gould's son, John, became the third generation to enter the family business, joined by his wife, Barbara, and their four children.

Eventually, because of the cost of coal, now at $10.00 a ton, and the lack of steady employees, operations at the greenhouse ceased in 1967. Many of the company's original employees had worked there for thirty to fifty years.

With the close of the Albion and Medina shops, concentration was on the Lockport location at 83 Locust Street. The Christmas Boutique, "The Added Touch," was opened in 1990 specializing in silk decorations in designer colors and the all-time favorites, red and green.

Glaser Corporation

Glaser Corporation was based in Middleport for nearly twenty years before re-locating at 1 Elizabeth Street in 1991, as the growing operation ran out of space at their facility in Medina, said Donald Coe, president. The new building offers 14,000 square foot of workspace.

The company produced tool management systems and tool presetting storage and design for other companies, as well as setting up computer software and hardware systems. Their work included the manufacture of cutting tools for the automotive industry, doing work for most of the major auto companies. In 1986, they were named the exclusive sales representative in western and central New York for the assembly equipment of the Wellman Co., of Medford, Massachusetts. The company had been owned by Harry Glaser, originally from Elmira.

Devpro Machine Inc.

Devpro was founded in 1972 by President Donald R. Coe, who designed and produced special machinery for drilling, milling and grinding, mainly for heavy industrial customers. FMC and Simons Steel, Lockport, were among their first customers. They produced heavy-duty conveyors for steel rolling mills, and conveyors and lift systems for automotive stamping plants.

Located in a 7,000 square foot building on Elizabeth Street, in 1980 they moved to the former Loud & Wendel plant on Route 31. Devpro started turning out tool-gauge and tool-control systems at their 18,000 square foot facility at 80 Telegraph Road, incorporating storage and tool-setting features which helped them to grow in the out-of-state market, with sixteen sales agents. Employment at the plant was twenty-five workers.

Devpro Machine was awarded an on-the-job training contract to hire two unemployed persons for training as tool and die makers.

In 1982 they purchased the manufacturing and distribution rights for a line of electrocutors and non-electric fly traps from the Detjen Corp. of Clinton Corners, New York. Models range from the small patio lantern style to the large industrial model used by farmers and dairies and large paper mills.

The plant was purchased in 1987 by Janak Trivedi. Operations were expanded to include compression molding of plastic parts. Devpro was led by Govin T. Rajan as president; the previous owner Richard C. Pfohl as vice-president, and Donald R. Coe, founder, as sales manager.

Middleport Manufacturing Company

The Middleport Manufacturing Company was organized in 1891 with the following leaders: George W. Eddy, president; James Compton, vice-president; George D. Judson, attorney and secretary, and L. S. Freeman, treasurer. A. E. Park was manager. They made window sashes, doors, blinds, and shutters, all inside furnishings for the eastern markets.

The Village Historian's office has two embroidery transfer patterns, one of birds and one of a girl and flowers, and stamped "Compliments of the Middleport Manufacturing Company, May 5, 1891."

Blinds, or wooden shutters, were used to conserve heat in the winter and to protect draperies from the summer sun. In pioneer days heavy wooden shutters were common as protection against marauders and possible Indian attacks. The main building was two-story, 60 feet by 100 feet, with wings 30 feet by 40 feet and 10 feet by 18 feet. A turn-of-the-century newspaper wrote that the growth of the village from 1227 to 1431 inhabitants between 1890 - 1900 was due primarily to the new "sash and blind" factory, as it was referred to locally. The old factory burned in 1895 and was rebuilt, but it closed in 1886.

R. M. Hughes & Vinegar Works

In the fall of 1909, work started on a huge vinegar works on the south side of Park Avenue near the railroad, the driveway between #36 and #38. The plant was on the east side of the drive. The plant employed men and processed 2000 bushel of apples per day; a bottling plant was built in 1924.

The plant was destroyed by fire, and a 1931 map shows Vinegar Work #2, and storage tanks with a capacity of 396,000 gallons.

In 1932, forty-eight barrels of vinegar were shipped from Middleport by accident in old spray barrels - they were seized in Pittsburgh. The Niagara Sprayer plant and their dock were very nearby.

The main Hughes factory was in Louisville, Kentucky, with branches in San Antonio, Texas, Savannah, Georgia, and Los Angeles, California.

R.M. Hughes had a vinegar plant located behind the present-day Norco building along the railroad tracks. The plant was destroyed by fire.
(Image from RTH)

Ontario Preserving Company, Batavia Preserving Company

The Ontario Preserving Company was organized in 1883 in the burned out building that had been the Buel P. Barnes flour mill. The walls of the four-story building on the north side of the canal at Mill & North Hartland Streets were six-feet wide at the base, tapering to twenty-inches wide at the top. With the installation of floors, windows, a roof, and the necessary processing machinery, the canning factory was ready for use. Power was by a water wheel, the water coming from a pond on the south side of the canal through an ease-way running under the canal.

Mr. Charles Francis was manager; Mr. Burt, Secretary-Treasurer, and Mr. J. S. Vary was superintendent, processor and chemist. Most of the recipes were Mr. Vary's ideas. All steam gauges, thermometers, etc. were marked in code, and scales were offset, so that a competitor world not be able to learn their methods of processing and preserving. Two threshing machine engines supplied steam for cooking and processing, until a boiler room was built.

The Ontario Preserving Company was the original name of the canning factory located on the north side of canal along Mill Street. It depended on the canal for water to run its machines.
(Image from MVH)

In 1894 another building was added to the boiler room to house the high-pressure steam retorts for the tin cans, and open vats where the glass jars were processed. Another small building was added to house a gasoline unit to provide gas for the fire pots in the main building, and to heat the soldering irons to make and seal the tin cans.

The first acetylene gas unit in the village was installed in the building, replacing the kerosene lamps. A few years later a gentleman was sent from Chicago to manage the company's office; he donated one of the units to the Methodist church for lighting.

For two years the Ontario Preserving Company packed peas. Farmers picked the pods from the vines; they were delivered to homes throughout the village and the women shelled them at home. Horse drawn wagons would collect the peas by noon so that they could be processed that day. Later, a pea shelling machine that resembled a small hand-cranked, two-rubber roll, cloth wringer was clamped to a table, and one pod at a time was fed into the machine, pushing the peas from the pod. Due to the high cost, the processing of peas was discontinued.

The company grew, and in 1891 a two-story building was added to the east of the original stone building. An ice house was constructed in which the stored fruits were kept cool. This was replaced by the first ammonia ice machine in the village, powered by a steam engine instead of using ice cut from the canal.

Produce ready for canning waiting to be delivered to the canning factory. Fruits and vegetables from area farms as well as some from as far away as Hawaii came to the factory to be preserved and then sent throughout the country.
(Image from MVH)

The largest percentage of the plant's pack was put into glass containers. Carloads of pineapple came from Hawaii, large red navel oranges came from Florida, strawberries came from Maryland, cherries, apricots and pears, and egg plums came from Canada. Fresh cranberries arrived in barrels; three gallon tins of figs for preserves; citron, raisins, currants, spices came for plum pudding and mincemeat; carloads of chicken and hams came for potted ham. Honey butter in five-gallon cans for red kidney beans arrived via the railroad and by local farmers and teamsters. Hundreds of barrels of sugar arrived here by canal from New York City. Glazed and sugar-coated fruits, Boston baked beans and kidney beans (the only vegetables packed here) were also packed under the Ontario Preserving label here at Middleport.

The first sprinkler system in the village was installed for fire protection. A large high pressure steam water pump was connected to a reservoir near the creek for its water supply; a 20,000-gallon water tank was placed on the roof in case the pump failed to work. Two canal steam packet boats from Medina and Gasport brought extra help to the factory each day.

More space was needed because of the increasing demand for more glass-packed preserves. In 1900, a three-story building was erected over the water wheel raceway on the north side of Mill Street, connected to the original building by an over-head, two-deck bridge. Only glass packed goods were handled in the new building, doubling the production wooden boxes were manufactured on the third floor for storing and shipping the canned goods.

A larger factory was needed to meet the demands of the now Batavia Preserving Company, so named by its new owners from Chicago.
(Image from MVH)

In 1891 the largest customer, Sprague-Warner Company of Chicago, bought the plant and the name was changed to Batavia Preserving Company. At this time, Jay S. Vary was transferred to the new Batavia, New York, plant and his son, Walter J. Vary, became the superintendent at Middleport. Wire snap-sealing unit invented by Jay S. Vary, and manufactured by the thousands but never patented. It was made on small, hand-operated machines. These fasteners are still used by Atlas, Ball and Mason canning jars.

In 1913, the Village Board notified the company that a meeting would be held regarding taxes and their assessment. It was about this time that the Village water works and Village sewer plant were being completed; possibly this was the reason for the increased assessments etc. Three officials from the Chicago office came, and after several unsuccessful meetings they threatened closure. The Village Attorney then told them that if they didn't want to go along with the original plan, that Middleport didn't need the Preserving Company. After a twenty-four-hour grace period, the plant closed its doors. The village not only lost its largest and fast growing industry employing 400 people, but also lost a potential glass and box factory.

A lot of the older employees were thrown out of work. However, some of them were transferred to the Batavia and Brockport plants. The farmers and fruit growers who had been producing fruits for the preserving department had no market for their products as the new owners discontinued the preserving department.

Known only to the officials of the company, plans had been completed to enlarge the preserving building and to build a factory to manufacture their own glass containers, as well as a box factory to manufacture boxes for the glass jars. Preserves, jams, jellies, mint and pudding sauces and glazed fruits were packed in all shapes and sizes of glass jars.

Plans were also under way to purchase all the land between Wildcat Creek and Hartland Street and north to the flour mill, for the new factory. The American Can Company sent their new sealing machines here in the wintertime to be tested under working conditions, as the Middleport plant was the only canning factory in Western New York that ran the year around.

They were to have a glass-making machine, a cut-glass machine and a tumbler engraving machine brought from Chicago and installed in the new factory here. The tumblers engraved with different designs would be used as drinking glasses when empty - a new idea to be advertised. A crew of twenty-five experienced glass machine operators would have been required to put the plant in operation, with more to be added when manufacturing began. Plant Superintendent Walter J. Vary went to Florida in 1912 to get samples and made arrangements to have white sand shipped here to be used in the glass manufacturing

The New York Central Railroad had to enlarge the freight yard here to handle the cars carrying goods to and from the factory.

Western New York fruit was considered to have better flavor and contained more fruit sugar than any other area of the state, creating a great demand for the Batavia Preserving Company jams and jellies. Batavia Preserving Company had its own stores located in many cities of the United States: stocks of their brands "Ferndale" and "Riehlieu" were well known to housewives. The Franchell store in Medina was a "Ferndale" store.

Batavia Preserving Company was followed by Bewley Brothers, and then by Longview Farms, operating as canning factories until 1967.

Middleport Flour Mill

The Middleport flour mill at the southwest corner of N. Hartland St. and Sherman Road was built in 1856 by Buel Barnes, one of the oldest millers in the state having been in the business since 1842. The four-story stone mill originally was powered by a water wheel.

Known as the "Lower Mills," or "Hartland Mills," after the death of Mr. Barnes it was operated by John F. Little & Son, before being purchased by the Thompson Milling Co. of Lockport, making "Angelus," "Pride of Niagara," and "Snow White Pastry Flour."

It was news in 1887 when a carload of flour was shipped in barrels, as cooper George Smith was making a very tight barrel, the first in using a locking rack-hoop requiring no nails. The building had not been used for at least forty years and was demolished in 1988 because of its deteriorating condition. With the advent of new technology and new methods of milling, the facility had become obsolete.

*The flour mill started on the southwest corner of N.
Hartland and Sherman Road, using the water from the
Wildcat Creek to turn its water wheel. The mill was
demolished in 1988.
(Image from Harold Mufford)*

Hartland Paper Company

The Hartland Paper Company was organized in about 1870 by Henry McClean, Jr., and Allen H. Pierce, producing a very good grade of straw paper. They employed twenty-three people with a payroll of $200 per week. In a few years it was totally destroyed by fire and rebuilt, located at the southwest corner of N. Hartland Street and Chase Road. In 1884 with Messers Eddy & Rowley, William J. Sterritt purchased the property and reorganizing as sole owner. The plant ran day and night, making waterproof straw wrapping paper. In 1891, the Hartland Paper Company was incorporated for the manufacture of box boards with a capacity of 2,500 ton per year. Colored pulp lined boxboard was a specialty.

The company failed in 1901 and merged into the United Box Board & Paper Co., a huge corporation with many plants throughout the country, capitalized at nearly $30 million. On May 8, 1903, the paper company was destroyed by a $50,000 fire.

Philleo & Pollard,
W. F. Pollard & Company

In 1881 the Middleport Industrial Chart, on which is sketched various business firms centered with the faces of the corresponding businessmen, was done by artists "Philleo and Pollard, Designers and practical artists, Middleport, NY."

W. F. (Floyd) Pollard, the son of James Pollard of Maple Avenue, and Arthur W. Whittaker, Francis Street, formed W. F. Pollard & Company for the purpose of making cartoons and commercial advertising engravings.

After doing various engraving works locally, including catalogues for the E. J. Lewis pineapple paring machine, and Edgar Knapp's Giant Bean picker, and the Thompson Milling Company, in about 1893 they headed for the West Coast in search of greener pastures. They stopped for short times in many cities to do engraving work; one of the more notable was "Last Chance Gold Mine" at Last Chance Gulch near Helena, Montana, one of the great gold strikes of the 1800s.

They finally landed in Spokane, Washington, where they opened an office and did the first newspaper illustration work north of San Francisco and west of Denver. They used the old chalk plate process and later the photo engraving process, to provide cartoons and pictures for two daily and about four weekly papers in that area. After a few years they sold out to the Spokane "Spokesman Review," the largest paper in the area. Pollard remained with the paper; Whittaker took a trip to Alaska to see the great phenomenon, the Muir Glacier, and returned to Middleport where he died in 1954 at the age of 79.

Pollard, who patterned his work after Thomas Nast, the famous cartoonist with Harper's Weekly in the 1870s, died in about 1946 at the age of 88 in Hemet, California, where he had lived for many years.

The Middleport Industrial Chart created by Philleo and Pollard, showing all the businesses in the village around 1881.
(Image from MVH)

Acknowledgments

First, I must thank Anna for her tireless effort in collecting, organizing, and documenting the history of Middleport. Without her stories and recollections, this book would not have been possible.

Mike Miller who walked me through the stages of getting this manuscript into book form.

Vicky Demmin, Rebecca Schweigert, and Sonora Miller for patiently editing the text.

All the people and organizations listed who provided me with photos, but especially Jesse Bieber, Royalton Historian, who was more than generous with his collection.

The entire community of Middleport, whose support of the "Porches of Middleport" poster, helped to finance this project.

My very patient husband Larry who spent many lonely evenings and my son Brian, though living miles away, was always ready to walk me through any computer glitch that came my way.

Christa Lutz, Middleport Village Historian